Daphne Lambert is a nutritionist who has cooked, studied and written about food all her adult life. She was the chef and co-owner of an award-winning organic restaurant for over 20 years.

She is a founding member of Greencuisine Trust and brings her passion for food that truly nourishes body, mind and spirit together with diverse experiences in the world of food to her work as an educator within the Trust.

She is the author of *Little Red Gooseberries*, a collection of recipes from her organic restaurant, and the co-author of the award-winning *The Organic Baby & Toddler Cookbook*. She regularly contributes recipes and articles to books and magazines.

LIVING FOOD

a feast for soil and soul

Daphne Lambert

unbound

This edition first published in 2016

Unbound
6th Floor Mutual House 70 Conduit Street London W1S 2GF
www.unbound.co.uk

Text Design by Drew Turner

Grateful Acknowledgements to:

Campbell-McBride, Dr Natasha. Gut and Psychology Syndrome: *Natural Treatment for Autism, ADD/ADHD, Dyslexia, Dyspraxia, Depression, Schizophrenia*. Medinform Publishing (2010).

Campbell-McBride, Natasha. *Put Your Heart in Your Mouth: What Really Is Heart Disease and What Can We Do to Prevent and Even Reverse It*. Medinform (2007).

Fukuoka, Masanobu. *The One-Straw Revolution: An Introduction to Natural Farming*. Rodale (1978).

Katz, Sandor. *Wild Fermentation: The Flavor, Nutrition, and Craft of Live-culture Foods*. Chelsea Green (2003).

Perlmutter, Dr David. *Brain Maker: The Power of Gut Microbes to Heal and Protect Your Brain – for Life*. Yellow Kite (2015).

Schulz, Andreas. *Water Crystals*. Floris Books (2005).

Schwenk, Theodor and Wolfram Schwenk. *Water: the element of life*. Anthroposophic Press (1989).

Young, Sera L., Paul W. Sherman, Julius B. Lucks, and Gretel H. Pelto. "Why On Earth?: Evaluating Hypotheses About The Physiological Functions Of Human Geophagy." *The Quarterly Review of Biology* 86.2 (2011): 97-120.

A CIP record for this book is available from the British Library

ISBN 978-1-78352-232-3 (trade hbk)
ISBN 978-1-78352-266-8 (ebook)
ISBN 978-1-78352-289-7 (limited edition)

Printed in Italy by L.E.G.O. S.p.A.

1 3 5 7 9 8 6 4 2

Dear Reader,

The book you are holding came about in a rather different way to most others. It was funded directly by readers through a new website: Unbound. Unbound is the creation of three writers. We started the company because we believed there had to be a better deal for both writers and readers. On the Unbound website, authors share the ideas for the books they want to write directly with readers. If enough of you support the book by pledging for it in advance, we produce a beautifully bound special subscribers' edition and distribute a regular edition and e-book wherever books are sold, in shops and online.

    This new way of publishing is actually a very old idea (Samuel Johnson funded his dictionary this way). We're just using the internet to build each writer a network of patrons. Here, at the back of this book, you'll find the names of all the people who made it happen.

    Publishing in this way means readers are no longer just passive consumers of the books they buy, and authors are free to write the books they really want. They get a much fairer return too – half the profits their books generate, rather than a tiny percentage of the cover price.

    If you're not yet a subscriber, we hope that you'll want to join our publishing revolution and have your name listed in one of our books in the future. To get you started, here is a £5 discount on your first pledge. Just visit unbound.com, make your pledge and type **livingfood** in the promo code box when you check out.

Thank you for your support,

Dan, Justin and John
Founders, Unbound

For Ben and Jess

Nutritional science has revealed to us how the nutrients in the food we eat can help keep us free from illness and grow to our full potential. Interpretations of this science have led to diverse opinions on the right diet to eat. Yes, we must consume lots of meat; no, we should all be vegan. Yes, lots of dairy is good for you; no, dairy should be avoided at all costs. Low-fat versus high-fat diets. Raw food versus cooked food. Ardent supporters of a particular regime highlight studies that show they are right; those opposed cite literature that categorically supports their position. While we have argued, diet-related chronic diseases have become the single largest cause of mortality in the West.

Indigenous people from around the world come from cultures placing value on 'knowing' without science: they simply 'know by being' what to eat. Diet-related chronic diseases are rare in these cultures, despite eating diets that many in the West would consider unhealthy. Clearly showing that no single diet suits all, high-grain, high-meat, high-dairy and high-fat diets can all be found, and what they have in common is that the foods are natural, sourced from an environment intimately known and prepared in ways that have been passed down from generation to generation. It is well documented that if an indigenous diet changes to a Western one of processed foods, health deteriorates. Traditionally, the diet of the Inuits was sea and land mammals, fish and birds with 75% of their calories coming from fat. Consumption of these traditional foods has declined since the arrival of processed food. Studies show that there has been a dramatic deterioration in the health and social structures of the Inuit culture.

Okinawans are the indigenous people of a Southern Japanese island. Their traditional diet, rich in complex carbohydrates, includes fresh vegetables and whole grains with the addition of fish, seaweed and tofu. Okinawans' lives are known for their longevity, with many citizens reaching the age of 100 still vibrant and engaged with life. At the end of the Second World War, US military troops moved in to Okinawa and fast food outlets quickly followed. As a result, younger Okinawans began to eat a processed diet. The younger generation now has the highest levels of obesity in Japan and are more likely to die of a heart attack and cancer than their elders.

We follow health gurus and particular diets with the promise of an ideal body weight, clearer thoughts, boundless energy, balance and health. We are persuaded by food industry marketing slogans to eat foods that do not nourish us. All too often, we forget the bigger picture. Food is about relationships. Relationships to soil, plants, animals, to each other and to the beautiful planet we live on. If we create loving relationships with the world around us, our choice of food becomes not just about individual health, but the long term health of the planet too. To reach decisions, Native American Haudenosaunee ask the question, 'what impact will this have on the seventh generation from today?'. It seems to me that in this enquiry is the bigger picture.

I have been fortunate to grow, harvest, prepare, share and love food all my life. On this journey there has been much pondering about what truly nourishes us. Eating food grown in vital soil you have rubbed between your fingers, land you have walked and from growers whose story you know is deeply nourishing – because it is about food that brings health to both yourself and the planet.

Living Food is the result of my life with food. It is a book to dip in and out of as it moves through the seasons of nature and the stages of human life. It is a journey from soil to soul, with recipes to enjoy along the way.

Daphne Lambert

I remember the first time I met Daphne, with the shock of red in her hair – a bit of a rock chick with a fierce love of the Earth. I was struck by her passion to explore and share the connection between the food we grow and eat and the well-being of all life on Earth. For a long time now we have known that the connection between health, well-being and ability to excel in life, whatever your purpose or persuasion, has a direct correlation with what we choose to eat. Daphne has spent over 40 years tapping into what can only be called Earth Nutrition. This book is pure rock and soil: the rocks are nuggets of wisdom, while the soil is what nourishes our food, and by extension, us.

Daphne has a lot to say about soil – and rightly so. As an Earth Nutritionist, she takes us on a journey through the very humus of life (quite literally, as the word human comes from the word humus) and, as she rightly points out, to be human is to be 'of the soil.' Herein lies the journey from soil to soul.

The very word nutrition comes from the word nutrire: feed, nourish. For Daphne, this is not about bare survival, nor is it about food per se: it is so much more. This book represents a wisdom I have been lucky to receive from Daphne over the last few years, and that now so many others will also be able to receive, too. More and more, the choices we make about our food speak of our values – do we value the Earth and how she is treated, or is it simply a matter of filling a trolley with whatever pre-packaged and processed item that first comes to hand? There is a deeper enquiry here; not just about where we choose to shop and what we choose to buy, but how we interact with community – our Earth community. It is an abuse to intensively farm and use herbicides and sprays that cause significant harm in the long term: to the land, the water, the atmosphere, our health and the well-being of us all.

By consciously choosing to de-couple from the ecocide that is intensive industrialised agriculture, we can and do support local, decentralised, beyond-organic food production. At a deeper level we are revering life itself – the life of our farm workers, our friends, our local market stall holders and all those who go to great effort to ensure what they sell is not carrying forward a legacy of harm. It's a political act of the highest form to feed one another food that is not being grown as a commodity. It is an act of deep care to feed our friends and family with food that comes from a healthy and thriving land, one that lives in the greatest freedom of all – a land that is free to be.

Polly Higgins
Earth lawyer and advocate for Ecocide law

LIVING FOOD

recipes and ingredients

The recipes in Living Food are generally simple and I am sure most of the ingredients will be familiar. Each recipe section uses UK seasonal produce with a smattering of ingredients from around the world including cacao, avocado, lemons, nuts, dates and spices. I encourage you to source organic and local from family or community farms and to be sure of the provenance of any products you use such as vinegar, olives, dried tomatoes and oils.

Recipes that contain gluten, soya, nuts, dairy and eggs are marked for those who avoid these ingredients.

There are a few recipes that use wheat and half a dozen or so that use unrefined sugar: I make no apologies for this! Many people can eat wheat with no adverse effects and a little sweetness can bring immense pleasure – just be attentive to the individual needs of your body.

Recipes are never cast in stone. Add, omit, change, be inspired – but most of all, enjoy.

What is local?
'Local' can be a bit undefined; it refers to food grown within a certain area, the size of which will differ depending on where you live. Some people live near more agriculturally productive areas than others, and it's possible to source all you need close at hand. For others, especially those living in cities, it's more difficult. It can be easier to start with UK produce, and then, as you build up knowledge through farmers markets, begin to source some produce closer to home.

What about the global food system?
We all love foods from around the world. However, one of the problems that arises when distant markets supply us with produce that is not a necessity is that this cash crop takes precedence over supplying local and regional provision to the inhabitants of a particular area. Transporting food around the world comes at a cost; however, our global food system may well be imperative in

years to come as climate change affects the ability of some people to successfully grow their own food. Global support will be needed to ensure that those living in these countries have enough to eat.

Why family or community farms?
Small scale family or community farms are central to food security, which a recent UN report on small scale organic farming confirms. Support for small farmers who follow agro-ecological practices is essential, as they are a vital key to the economic and environmental challenges we face in the future.

What is food provenance?
Food provenance is knowing where your food comes from. When you buy from knowledgeable people you learn the stories behind your food. Knowledge of food provenance allays fears around human rights abuses, use of chemicals, cheap filler ingredients and animal welfare.

Which preserved foods are best?
Preserved foods made using traditional artisan methods support a vital way of life. Often made on or close to the farm where the ingredients are grown, these products capture food at its most flavoursome, minimise waste and extend its availability.

contents

Introduction by Daphne Lambert – 9
Foreword –11

A Feast for Soil and Soul – 18

Spring
  Digestion – 46
  Conception and Birth – 51
  Nutrients for Conception – 54
  Smoothies for Mums to be – 56
  The Acid and Alkaline – 58
  Juicing – 62
  Sprouts and Sprout Greens – 67
  Wheatgrass Juice – 70
  Seven Flavours of Spring – 72
  Spring Health from the Meadows and Hedgerows
        Romy Fraser – 75
  Spring Recipes – 78

Summer
  Dairy – 96
  Good and Bad Fats – 104
  Sugar – 111
  Dancing Hormones – 117
  Nourishing Families – 120
  Family Breakfasts – 124
  Grow, Cook, Share – 130
  Seven Flavours of Summer – 132
  The Industrialisation of Soya and Corn
        Diane Osgood – 135
  Summer Recipes – 138

Autumn

    Healthy Immune System – 158
    The Immune System Glossary – 162
    Immune-strengthening Salads – 164
    Rainbow Foods – 168
    Healing Power of Plants – 172
    Taste – 174
    Fermenting – 176
    Food and Community – 184
    Seven Flavours of Autumn – 186
    Revitalising Ritual, Every Day, Every Mouthful
        Miche Fabre Lewin – 189
    Autumn Recipes – 192

Winter

    Growing Food – 213
    Later Years – 222
    Nourishing Meals in a Bowl – 226
    Sea Vegetables – 232
    Water – The Gift of Life – 236
    At-a-glance Vitamins and Minerals – 244
    Seven Flavours of Winter – 246
    Sharing Goodness
        Sandra White – 249
    Winter Recipes – 252

Acknowledgements – 268
Recipe Index – 269
Supporters – 276

a feast for
soil and soul

*'The soil is the great connector of our lives, the
source and destination of all.' – Wendell Berry*

From soil we come, to soil we return – and as we journey, soil, the living crust of planet Earth, feeds us via plants and animals. We are inextricably linked to the soil. To be human is to be 'of the soil'.

For much of human history the life-giving bond between people and soil was commonly understood. As we have moved away from a rural way of living towards an urban one, we have become physically, socially and spiritually removed from the soil.

Primitive man evolved eating food from the landscape; then, around 10,000 years ago, the nomadic hunter-gatherer culture began to settle and agriculture emerged. Farmers raised plants and animals for food, and anything grown surplus to their needs was traded with those who lived in nearby towns and villages.

Today, more than half of the world's population live in towns and cities, and it is estimated that two-thirds of the world's population will become urban dwellers by 2050. Urban living creates a lack of connection to soil, and this is a separation that affects us on many levels. Gandhi expressed this loss when he said, 'To forget how to dig the earth and tend the soil is to forget ourselves.'

Up until relatively recently, eating raw fruit and vegetables from the fields or directly from family gardens was commonplace, and ingesting soil-based organisms with the food we ate would have been the norm – simply because of the way we grew, harvested and prepared our own food. Our modern-day food industry destroys most of these organisms, and this, together with our excessively clean households, means few (if any) of these soil-based organisms manage to find their way into the human digestive tract. There is evidence to suggest that the ingestion of soil-based organisms from a vibrant, healthy soil enhances the functioning of our gastrointestinal tract, but mostly we have lost the relationship between the soil of the land and the soil of our being: our gut.

It is well recorded that many cultures practise geophagy, or soil eating. The first written documentation dates back to the Greek physician Hippocrates (460 BC). Eating soil in one form or another has been seen on every continent and in nearly every country, from small balls of local earth carried by Siberian tribes to nibble on their travels, to earth processed by termites eaten by women from

West Africa. It had been thought that soil was eaten for its mineral content; however, Sera Young of Cornell University analysed data and found this a very unlikely hypothesis. Her research concluded that the far more likely reason for people eating soil was for the support it gave to the digestive tract.

The ancient Egyptians ate soil to treat various ailments, especially for healing the gut. Today the French in particular are still great believers in eating *argile* (clay): they use it to stimulate the immune system and remove toxins from the body. Clay eating during the early stages of pregnancy and by young children is a well-known practice and has a soothing effect on the stomach.

Soil-based organisms, once ingested, pass through the stomach and form colonies of beneficial bacteria in the digestive tract; there they restore and maintain a healthy bacterial environment by consuming waste materials and encouraging the growth of other beneficial bacteria. One of the great advantages of soil-based organisms is that they are extremely robust and able to survive the acidity of the stomach.

'To forget how to dig the earth and tend the soil is to forget ourselves.' – Gandhi

Both soil and our intestines depend on bacteria to flourish. A living soil is rich in friendly bacteria and microbes, which help plants grow vital and strong. Likewise, our gut, teeming with up to 100 trillion microbes – known as our gut microbiota, supports our growth. Bacteria are very active in the colon, making this the site where more metabolic activity takes place than in any other organ in the body, similar to the activity that takes place in the top few inches of soil. And they are vital: neither humans nor plants can absorb nutrients without the help of bacteria.

One-third of our gut microbiota is common to most people, while two-thirds are specific to individuals determined by genetics, our environment and the food we eat. Maintaining a healthy, balanced gut microbiota is the key to vibrant health. These beneficial microorganisms perform many tasks, including creating a physical barrier on the surface of the gut wall to prevent undigested food, toxins and parasites from moving through the permeable wall into the body and causing a myriad of problems, helping to digest certain foods that the stomach and small intestine have not been able to digest, and helping with the production of some vitamins, such as B and K.

Exposure to a wide range of bacteria, especially during infancy, stimulates the immune system. Soil-based organisms help to strengthen immunity, which is why early childhood contact with healthy soil is so beneficial. Many nutritionists speculate that lack of exposure to soil is one of the contributory factors to the alarming increase in allergies. There is also a hypothesis that reduced exposure to soil-based organisms could be responsible for an array of other gut disorders and immune-related disease.

'The gut microbiome is 99% of the DNA in your body, and it is highly responsive and changeable based upon lifestyle choices, most importantly our food choices.' – Dr David Perlmutter

Research shows that there is a close correlation between gut bacteria and brain development, a condition nutrition expert Dr Natasha Campbell-McBride calls Gut and Psychology Syndrome (GAPS). Gut flora appears to be essential in maintaining brain function, and it influences a range of neurological conditions such as autism, attention deficit hyperactivity disorder (ADHD) and schizophrenia. Beneficial bacteria in your intestines maintain the integrity of the gut lining; once this becomes compromised, you can end up with a permeable gut wall, which increases inflammation, and this is a particular feature of virtually all brain disorders. The gut bacteria are involved in manufacturing the neurochemicals dopamine and serotonin, which help your mind stay calm and focused on a task and help you to resist depression and other mood disorders.

The delicate interrelationships that exist between the different microorganisms that live in the gut can be disrupted, leading to a variety of problems. Stress, an array of environmental hazards including pesticides, and non-steroidal anti-inflammatory drugs (NSAIDs) such as ibuprofen can seriously interfere with gut ecology, and antibiotics are prone to wipe out both the good and bad microorganisms, rendering the entire gut sterile. Refined foods, especially sugar, upset the gut by encouraging the growth of undesirable bacteria and yeasts, resulting in an imbalance of the gut microbiota. Dr David Perlmutter, a leading natural medicine neurologist in the US, says, 'The gut microbiome is 99% of the DNA in your body, and it is highly responsive and changeable based upon lifestyle choices, most importantly our food choices.'

Naturally grown foods, fresh in season or preserved by artisan traditions, especially probiotic lacto-fermented vegetables, along with prebiotic fibre (found in lots of vegetables, particularly onions, leeks, artichokes and asparagus) support good intestinal health.

Taking time to grow your own food in vibrant living soil in the garden, on an allotment, in a window box or even in pots on the doorstep is also a way of supporting good health. By severing our relationship with soil, we have broken bonds that have been tens of millions of years in the making. By renewing and nurturing this age-old relationship with soil, we invite in the very source of life.

'A nation that destroys its soil destroys itself.'
– Franklin Roosevelt

Fertile soil is an exquisite interplay of billions of organisms, and it is this microbial biodiversity that gives rise to the myriad forms of life that feed us. The complexity of rich, vibrant, organic soil is extraordinary. There are more microorganisms in a handful of this kind of soil than there are people in the world – up to a billion microorganisms from up to 10,000 species in just one teaspoon of soil!

Soil-based organisms are tiny microbes that live in soil. Their many functions include digesting inorganic substances; protecting root systems from harmful parasites, yeasts and fungi; and providing growth factors and different hormones. They support healthy plants by preventing contamination with undesirable organisms that are antagonistic to growth. Although very few of the microbial species in soil have been identified, it is known that they have evolved a complex symbiotic relationship with plants. Every bit of the plant produces food to promote the growth of bacteria and fungi and, in return, the bacteria release nutrients for the plant to grow – the fertility of the soil and its ability to grow healthy plant life depend to a large extent on the levels of organic matter within it. Organic material from plants, animals and organisms decomposes, and when this becomes resistant to any further decomposition, it is known as humus. Unlike organic material, humus is stable, creating a fertile soil which is extremely absorptive, holding and releasing water and nutrients as needed. It also improves the structure of soil so that it is crumbly and aerated. Without stable humus, along with decaying plant and animal matter, the soil cannot support the wide variety of organisms that enable nourishing food to be grown.

The use of chemical fertilisers, herbicides and pesticides has been shown to inhibit the microbiological life in the soil, which in turn affects the health of plants. Swiss researchers spent 21 years comparing the soil of organic and non-organic farming, and dramatic differences in the mass of soil organisms were found. On the organic land, the mass of microorganisms, which provide delivery of nutrients to the roots of crops, was 25% greater. In soils treated with pesticides, there were 60–90% fewer earthworms, essential for aerating, draining and fertilising.

The use of soluble nitrogen fertiliser results in a higher nitrogen concentration in the plant sap and thinner cell walls, increasing the susceptibility of crops to pests and diseases. When a plant is deprived of the nutrition it needs to flourish, it suffers from a depleted immune system, and this in turn diminishes the ability of the plant to nourish anything that eats it.

Soil fertility affects the vitality of plants and plays an essential role in the water cycle, storing carbon and mitigating the effects of climate change. The more fertile the soil, the more water is able to infiltrate the Earth's crust and, as it slowly percolates down to the aquifer, it is purified by microorganisms on its journey. When soil lacks fertility, water will run off the land into rivers and waterways, at the same time taking with it valuable topsoil. The formation of just one inch of topsoil takes around 500 years on agriculturally used land – we cannot afford to lose this valuable soil.

Water is a major global concern; climate change results in both increased rainfall and drought. Organic soils are able to absorb large amounts of heavy rainwater without waterlogging or erosion, and in a drought these soils are more capable of storing available water, creating a greater resilience, which is vital for global food security.

Soil is an important carbon store, and it is very important to keep soil carbon where it is to help minimise the build-up in the atmosphere of greenhouse gases. Soil sequestration of carbon is therefore very important in helping to mitigate climate change. Soil sequestration is the process of transferring carbon dioxide from the atmosphere into the soil. Through photosynthesis, a plant draws carbon out of the air to form carbon compounds. What the plant doesn't need for growth is exuded through the roots to feed soil organisms, whereby the carbon is rendered stable. The degradation of soils from unsustainable agriculture through exposure and erosion has released billions of tonnes of carbon into the atmosphere.

Thirty years of Rodale Institute soil carbon data has clearly shown the benefits of natural farming to carbon sequestration. Reduced tillage and systems that do not use artificial fertilisers, adding instead high amounts of biomass to the soil through composting and crop rotation, have a greater ability, they have shown, to sequester carbon.

How soil carbon is leached from the earth and how that process can be reversed is the subject of much research, with major implications in helping to slow the rapid rise of carbon dioxide in the atmosphere. Soils with the highest carbon stores are forests, peat lands and carbon-rich pastures. Unsuitable land-management practices such as the draining of peat lands, forest clearing and converting pasture into arable land can have devastating effects on maintaining soil carbon stocks. Globally, about 47% of emissions from agriculture still come from releasing CO_2 by converting land to agricultural use; clearing rainforest to rear livestock, for example, releases CO_2 into the atmosphere.

Looking after our soils is critical for our survival. It is often argued that industrial intervention is necessary to grow enough food to feed our growing population. Bill Liebhardt from the University of California, Davis, found that yields of organic corn were 94% of conventional yields, but another example of organic tomatoes showed no yield difference. Swiss research found that there could be up to 20% less yield on organic farms. However, in poorer nations, Jules Pretty and Rachel Hine – when they researched over 200 agricultural projects converting to an ecological approach – found a dramatic increase in yield. Even if yields were lower, it would not matter in terms of the long-term disruption to the living matter in soil of chemical farming.

Soil is integral to every living system. Without soil, life as we know it would simply not exist. We are dependent on soil; it is the planet's fragile skin of soil that anchors our life on Earth.

'At the deepest level of ecological awareness you are talking about spiritual awareness. Spiritual awareness is an understanding of being embedded in a larger whole, a cosmic whole, of belonging to the universe.' – Fritjof Capra

Over the last 10,000 years and exponentially in the last 75 years, humans have made an ever-increasing impact on the planet's ecosystems. Our view of the world tends to be very human-centred. We seem to forget that there are many species living on Earth, and together they form an interconnected living system. On the whole, we ignore how our human actions are having a profound effect on the well-being of all the Earth's inhabitants.

Food shapes our world and, whatever way you look at it, the impact of the food we eat is enormous, encompassing pretty much all contemporary economic, environmental, social, political and health challenges. However, with every mouthful we have the opportunity to fully engage with the nature of our impact and, in so doing, bring about a deeper appreciation of our place in the world. When we start to truly understand where our food comes from, we become aware of how everything is interconnected and how the choices we make affect the entire web of life.

By giving greater consideration to the food we eat, a deeper understanding grows of the ethical implications, social consequences and environmental effects of each food choice. Many foods, especially the abundant, cheap, processed foods, hide the true environmental and social cost of our current dominant food and agricultural system. Each stage of food production from farming to storage, transport, processing and packaging results in greenhouse gas emissions. Deforestation, overconsumption of water, loss of biodiversity and pollution from industrial farming are some of the environmental impacts that can be hidden in the food on your plate. The social costs of bringing food to the table can also be significant, including land conflicts, human rights violations, loss of homes and livelihoods, the impoverishment of rural communities, and non-communicable diseases such as diabetes and cardiovascular disease.

The industrialisation of food and farming has resulted in too much power in the hands of just a few large corporations, which are able to control how food is produced and traded. There is a growing realisation that the alienation from the source of our food needs to change and it is necessary – indeed, vital – to move towards methods of farming and eating that honour the interconnectedness of all life. Family and small-scale farms are at the heart of this movement for change; they are farmers who, through relationships with their local ecosystem and the people who buy and share their produce, are inextricably linked to supporting planetary and human health.

We cannot view food as a commodity simply to be traded for profit. It is vital that farms meet, as far as is possible, the needs of people living close by, and this should take precedence over export-orientated agriculture.

Research shows that it is not large-scale monocultures but small farms that are key to food security; these farms are rich sanctuaries for biodiversity, producing sustainable food that contributes to thriving local economies and a sustainable way of living, which also do not negate the possibility of accessing healthy, ethically produced and affordable food. Throughout the UK there are box schemes bringing freshly harvested seasonal produce into the hearts of cities. In addition, there are so many community food projects to engage with, including city farms, community gardens, food cooperatives and community meals. By engaging with these initiatives, you are helping to ensure that food in your community is healthy and of benefit to everyone.

Manufactured and cheap foods contribute to a world view that humans are the most important form of life on this planet. These foods give little heed to protecting the diversity of plants or the needs of animals. In addition, the energy-intensive industrial methods that are used damage the environment and dwindle away Earth's natural resources. Seasonal, organic produce, sourced fresh and as locally as possible, together with preserved artisan products that are made observing traditional wisdoms, acknowledge our inter-being with the Earth. These foods help support local economies and enable sustainable livelihoods to thrive; they contribute to mitigating against climate change and avoid destroying the natural resources of the planet.

By being mindful about what we eat, we become aware of how nourishing ourselves and nourishing the Earth go hand in hand.

The same stream of life that runs through my veins night and day runs through the world and dances in rhythmic measures.

It is the same life that shoots in joy through the dust of the earth in numberless blades of grass and breaks into tumultuous waves of leaves and flowers.

It is the same life that is rocked in the ocean cradle of birth and death, in ebb and flow.

I feel my limbs are made glorious by the touch of this world of life. And my pride is from the life throb of ages dancing in my blood this moment.

– Rabrindranath Tagore

*'Simplicity requires less ego and more imagination,
less complication and more creativity, less
glamour and more gratitude, less attention to
appearance and more attention to essence.'
– Satish Kumar*

To maintain the integrity and beauty of planet Earth, we must find
ways to reduce our ecological impact on the planet. With economic
breakdown, resource depletion and climate change already
underway, some may argue that the tipping point has arrived. New
ways of living are needed; if all of the peoples of the world were
to adopt the modern Western consumer lifestyle, we would need
five planets on which to live. I trust that there is still a window of
opportunity for change, but there can be no doubt that we must
act quickly.

In the Western world the global food system provides us with an
infinite variety of food and delivers an abundance of choice, mostly
through supermarkets, right into the heart of our communities.
Our year-round abundance carries a heavy price, though, ranging
from tomatoes grown out of season on artificial substrate to battery
chickens, from caged, chemically treated salmon to pesticide-soaked
vegetables, and the ever-increasing threat that looms over us of
genetic modification.

Suppliers of cheap, fast food, along with our perceived need for
'convenience', have, over the last 50 years, allowed industrial food
production to become part of our everyday lives. The global system
of multinational corporations has put itself into a position of control
over what we grow and manufacture, and the underlying driving
force is profit, not the provision of healthy food for everyone. This
system has created around a billion hungry people and, at the same
time, around two billion are obese or overweight. These figures
show how urgent it is to find the wisdom to change our relationship
with food so that we are all able to flourish well.

Facing this huge challenge can make us feel rather powerless
– but we are not. As individuals, families and communities we can
make decisions around the food we choose to eat that will make a
positive difference to ourselves and the world around us.

A sea change in attitudes around how we grow and what we eat
is already happening. Today, more and more people question the

validity of the practices of the industrial food supply. This groundswell prefers food grown nearby, rather than global commodities grown thousands of miles away, and supports inspirational, local food initiatives. Farmers' markets and sales direct from the farm gate have increased dramatically in the last ten years, offering seasonal, fresh produce.

Community Supported Agriculture schemes share both the responsibilities and rewards of farming. Allotments are thriving and demand far exceeds availability. Innovative ways of providing food are flourishing, including growing vegetables in schools, hospitals, community gardens, city centres, urban farms and on rooftops – choices are being made that are changing our world for the better.

Refined and highly processed foods are simply not appropriate for supporting energetic and spirited people thriving on a healthy planet.

> *From the weekly supermarket shop, take a pizza and remove it from the cardboard box, unwrap the plastic wrapper, remove the polystyrene base and pop the pizza into the microwave for two minutes; then eat the symbol of our convenience culture. The pizza may appear simple, but that is not the case – it has been produced through increasingly complex food chains at vast cost to the environment.*

Using as much fresh, local produce as you are able, along with global produce with clear traceability back to the farm, fosters a greater intimacy to soil, food and people and supports the planet's ecology.

> *A beetroot, earth still clinging to the root – dark green leaves with marbled red veins attached – arrives fresh from the community shared garden. Shred the leaves, wilt in oil and place into a bowl, then scrub the beetroot and grate. Mix with a little apple cider vinegar, olive oil and black pepper, pile on top of the leaves, scatter over hemp seeds and eat with crimson-stained hands. Taste the soil!*

We have been marketed a food consumer-orientated lifestyle, but we need to break away from the perception of ourselves as food consumers. It undermines the true value of our relationship with food. By being attentive to the whole food cycle, we become responsible for the well-being of ourselves, our communities and Earth. Through taking time to simply and lovingly prepare the food we eat, we connect more fully to the essence of that which nourishes us.

'What an extraordinary achievement for a civilization: to have developed the one diet that reliably makes its people sick!' – Michael Pollan

Like all creatures, we have evolved finding nourishment from whole foods gathered from our immediate environment. Unlike other creatures, however, humans discovered ways to process and fragment food, and the result is that many of the foods we eat today are missing both their life force and the synergy of their nutrients.

All living organisms have a life force that forms a vibrational frequency. This energy can either form a pattern of coherence or chaos. Dr Fritz Alfred Popp, a German physicist and founder of the International Institute of Biophysics in Neuss, showed that the life force, as a light emission from all living organisms, is an expression of health. He went on to show that the life force in the foods we eat has a profound effect on the coherence of our individual energy field, and therefore our health. Professor Hans Eppinger, who was the chief medical director of the first medical clinic at the University of Vienna, found that whole, live foods enhanced the electrical potential in our cells, thus strengthening our life force energy, while fragmented and over-processed cooked foods did not. Nobel Prize laureate Albert Szent-Györgyi described the vibrational energy in live food as 'a little electric current sent to us by the sunshine'. Live food is filled with these live electrons from the sun because living food has not had – through processing methods – its electron patterns disrupted.

In whole foods, living energy is integral and vibrant; once split apart, it is lost. Raw milk, apples and wheat grains are whole foods. Pasteurised skimmed milk, apple juice and white flour are not. Many elements have been refined out of the processed and fragmented foods we eat today, and we are missing important nutrients and fibre.

The food we eat can be prepared in a way that maintains the life force and nutrients, or it can be processed in a way that depletes the inherent energy along with the quality and quantity of nutrients. Modern methods of refining and processing have created life-depleting food that had the potential to be life-enhancing. Wheat grain is a good example: the grain is made up of three parts, the germ, which, given the right conditions, will sprout and give rise to the first tiny leaves and rootlets; the carbohydrate-rich endosperm, which provides energy and nourishes the seedling during its early growth before its leaves begin photosynthesis; and the bran, the outer covering that protects the grain. The germ is nutrient-rich, full of vitamins, oils and protein; the endosperm is predominately starch; and the bran contains fibre, minerals, protein and vitamins.

After harvesting, the dry whole wheat grains are stored. In this form, the wheat is dormant, with the potential for life. Soaking brings life back to the grain, while sprouting and fermenting enhance the life force as well as increasing the nutritional value. These time-honoured methods respect the energetics and nutritional synergy to be found in the whole grain.

When we grind wheat into flour, we destroy the potential of life in the grain, and the more the grain is processed, the more we lose both the quality and quantity of nutrients. In the late 1800s, steel rollers began to replace stone wheels and revolutionised turning wheat into flour as the process was able to separate both the bran and the germ from the endosperm, leaving pure white flour. White flour has a longer shelf life, a distinct advantage for the manufacturer and the retailer but disastrous in terms of nutrition. Up to 80% of the nutrients that are found in the whole wheat grain are lost when processed into a white flour. In particular, B vitamins thiamine (Vitamin B1) and niacin (Vitamin B3) are lost. Thiamine deficiency causes beriberi and niacin deficiency causes pellagra. When it was finally accepted that these were diseases of deficiency, fortification was introduced and synthetic B vitamins were added to white flour. This may have been beneficial in cases of severe insufficiency, but it did not address the importance of wholeness. We now know that refined grains, devoid of life force and nutrient synergy, contribute to the three major killers in modern society: coronary heart disease, diabetes and certain cancers.

It is not only the way we process grain that causes a problem. Today, many of the varieties of wheat we are eating have significantly lower nutritional content than the wheat varieties we used to grow. There are about 200,000 varieties of wheat the world over, with only a few genetic lines of wheat now feeding the world. Whilst some people have to avoid wheat altogether, others find that older varieties like kamut, spelt, emmer and einkorn are much easier to digest.

As older varieties of grains, vegetables and fruits – often referred to as heirloom – generally have a higher nutrient content than their modern counterparts, it is worth seeking them out, especially if you grow your own. Another reason to support heirloom varieties is that they represent a vast and diverse pool of genetic characteristics, one that will be lost forever if these plants are allowed to become extinct. Diversity is critical in the face of changing weather patterns. There are many different grains grown throughout the world, and it was growing, harvesting and storing grains to eat during periods when there was little food available that allowed civilisations to grow.

As well as drying and storing, there are many other ways of preserving food. Preserving stretches the period of availability of seasonal foods, and home preservation from the garden or from a local seasonal glut ensures preserving at the very peak of ripeness, maximum nutrition and, of course, avoiding waste.

Commercially there are two main kinds of food preservation: modern industrial food manufacturing and natural artisan methods. The major driver for industrial food processing is the creation of a convenience food with a good profit. Food in the hands of a technologist is likely to have been made using a potential palette of 6,000 food additives to make a creamier texture, give a better rise, look glossier, prolong shelf life – the list is endless. The artisan process is unhurried and reflects expertise, tradition and passion. Artisan producers know that the way food is farmed gives each food its individual taste, texture, smell, and the overall quality; how the grass a cow eats makes for a unique cheese or how the flavour of a tomato comes from the particular nutrients contained in the soil. Time-honoured methods make foods edible, like olives and capers, preserve foods at the peak of freshness and flavour, like bottled tomatoes and pesto, or improve the nutritional content, as is the case with lacto-fermentation.

A health-giving diet is based on organic whole foods, predominantly plant-based, with as much wild-harvested and locally grown as is possible; these foods together with artisan preservations will bring nourishing and life-enhancing food to the table.

We have evolved on planet Earth, living in the most diverse ecosystems and, until comparatively recently, eating foods sourced from our immediate environment. From the harsh, rugged landscape of the Australian Outback to the tangled mass of vegetation at the heart of the Amazon rainforest, from the white sands of the Sahara to the frozen landscape of Greenland, from the seascape of Polynesia to the soft green valleys of Wales, wherever we have settled, creating families and communities, nature has provided food to support us.

Through the ages across the world, specific food cultures have developed, each one determined by the knowledge of a particular region. However, in the last 200 years, dramatic changes have occurred in the way we eat, as industrial countries have become independent of geography, climate and season. Traditional cuisines are being replaced by new eating patterns fostered by new technologies, ways of living and economic structures. Today we have less understanding of how, as part of nature, our bodies work best when they harmonise with the food of the seasonal rhythms.

The ancient Chinese system saw how we, as part of nature, were influenced by the weather and how adjusting our lifestyle to mirror nature brought inner harmony. Spring is a time of rebirth; then, with renewed vitality, we are swept along on the wave of abundant growth to the radiant summer, season of wild creativity. Autumn is the time to accept and let go as everything begins to return to where it came from. In winter, we sink into a quiet and inward-oriented energy, a time for reflection and a deepening of our understanding of our purpose in the world.

Nature's seasons give us a beautiful rhythm to live by. The upward moving essence of spring creates tiny shoots of green energy – spring foods rejuvenate and help us cleanse the body. Salads made using young chickweed, yarrow and dandelion support cleansing, along with soups made from the glossy, dark green leaves of wild garlic, watercress and spinach. The first green shoots of asparagus, a gentle spring diuretic, poke through the soil, and tender nettles can be turned into cleansing green juices to revitalise the body. Sprouted seeds like broccoli and sunflower are powerhouses of life and energy and prepare us for the abundance of summer.

During the summer months, nature gives us a bedazzling array of colourful fruits and vegetables; apricots, strawberries, blackcurrants and raspberries are perfect to eat just the way they are. Brilliant yellow flowers on the ends of green courgettes, shiny red tomatoes, colourful peppers, orange carrots, delicate pink chives, showy red lettuce, pale green peas, cascades of orange flowers that become crisp, green runner beans, red chillies, smooth purple aubergine, golden orange nasturtium; brilliant colours that fire the imagination.

As the summer days shorten and the landscape changes to fiery reds, bronzes and golds, it is natural to turn to warming foods. In autumn, the harvest includes cabbage, sweetcorn, pumpkins, leeks, onions, garlic, mushrooms, pears, apples, figs, blackberries and rosehips; some can be turned into warm, fragrant meals of soups, casseroles and bakes, the rest preserved and stored. At this time of year everything in nature contracts and moves its essence inwards and downwards – the foods that are abundant at this time of year support us as we prepare for winter.

We all need a time to rest, and the cold dark days of winter encourage this process of slowing down. The foods that nourish us most during this reflective period are the dense-textured, earthy flavours of root crops like parsnip, swede, turnip, celeriac, beetroot, Jerusalem artichoke and potatoes. These, together with the winter crops of brassicas and chard and the salty flavour of sea vegetables, are the foods best suited to be eaten in the winter months.

Climate change is likely to affect the ability of some people to successfully grow their own food, leading to hunger and famine without global food support, but supplying distant markets with produce that is not a real necessity should not take precedence over local and regional provision.

If we break the magic of the seasonal alchemy by globally seeking foods that are out of season in our own environment and not essential to our needs, we forget that we are part of nature and create disorder in ourselves and the world around us.

'Soil is the connection to ourselves. From soil we come and to soil we return. If we are disconnected from it we are aliens adrift in a synthetic environment.' – Fred Kirschenmann

Cultures rich in traditional wisdom and knowledge have great reverence for the land and a deep understanding of the importance of soil, not only for the present but for past and future generations. In the Western culture, a feeling of connection to soil has been lost. The understanding that our past and future are tightly woven into soil barely exists. The cycle of life and death exists through soil. Today we have forgotten how we are bound to the land, and our daily dependence for survival has shifted away from a direct relationship with life-giving soil and entered an era of technological innovation and industrialisation. This, together with a belief that we are separate from nature and can do what we want with her without affecting ourselves, has driven us into reliance on systems that will destroy the precious soil that gives us life.

Holding soil in our hands connects us to the source of life and brings a spiritual connection to what it means to be alive. As Thomas Berry, the great 'earth scholar', so succinctly put it, 'It is impossible to contemplate the life of the soil for very long without seeing it as analogous to the life of the spirit'.

We are energetic beings and it is the soil that quite literally earths us. Did you know that when you put your bare feet on soil, you absorb a large number of negative electrons through the soles of your feet? To be grounded through a connection with soil brings about a strong sense of purpose concerning how we grow and what we choose to eat. These choices bring us to a place of presence, awareness and consciousness, and this is where we find soul.

Every day, when we eat healthy food, we are connected to vital soil. If we eat food prepared with mindfulness, appreciation and a loving consciousness, we are connected to soul; herein lies the journey from soil to soul.

Sowing the seed,
my hand is one with the Earth.
Wanting the seed to grow,
my mind is one with the light.
Hoeing the crop,
my hands are one with the rain.
Having cared for the plants,
my mind is one with the air.
Hungry and trusting,
my mind is one with the Earth.
Eating the fruit,
my body is one with the Earth.

– Wendell Berry

spring

digestion

Digestion begins with the engagement of the senses. Take a deep breath: smell, see, touch and listen to the food you are preparing in anticipation of the delight of the tastes to come. Fine slices of fennel cooked for a few seconds in olive oil – the first crunch releases the sweet aniseed flavour. The incredible aroma of a round, shiny, smooth red tomato picked warm from the plant, eaten sprinkled with salt, pepper, basil and olive oil – an explosion of flavour in your mouth. The texture and fragrance of mashed potato – succulent, soft and comforting. The sharp citrus smell from a slice of lemon – astringent and sour as you suck the juice. The sensuous fragrance of freshly harvested summer strawberries. Crisp apples, full of tart and refreshing pale green juice. The aroma of earthy mushrooms gathered from the floor of the woods, sizzling in a pan with sweet red onion and pungent garlic. Just thinking about food will bring saliva flowing into your mouth.

The magical transformation of food in our bodies begins in the mouth as we grind, crunch and munch what we are eating. The tongue moves the food about, mixing it with saliva, which is secreted into the mouth via salivary glands. As you chew, saliva helps to break down the food, moistening it and making it easier to swallow. Amylase, an important digestive enzyme in the saliva, begins to break down carbohydrates into simple sugars. Saliva also contains antibodies that fight bacteria. The thousands of taste buds in the tongue detect bitter, sour, sweet, salty, pungent and umami flavours. When the food is well masticated, it is swallowed down the oesophagus and into the stomach. The pleasure from tasting will have sent messages to the rest of the digestive system, and before the food reaches the stomach, gastric juices are flowing.

The muscles of the stomach churn and mash the food, mixing it around with gastric juice. This highly acidic environment is just right for breaking down protein. An average meal containing carbohydrates, protein and fats takes up to six hours to leave the stomach. The contents of the stomach – now known as chyme – move into the small intestine. The chyme is mixed with pancreatic juice, bile and intestinal juice, facilitating further breakdown of the food into simple molecules ready for absorption. The moist tissue – known as mucosa – that lines the walls of the small intestine contains many folds that are covered with tiny, finger-like

projections called villi, and covering them are epithelial cells, each of which is covered with microvilli. These cells, which are constantly being renewed to work efficiently, are the cells that complete the digestive process and absorb the nutrients from the food we eat. Carbohydrates, proteins and fats, all broken down into simple molecules, together with vitamins and minerals, pass through the wall of the intestine to be transported around the body. Food waste enters the large intestine through a one-way valve, where it becomes food for the bacteria that live there; amongst a host of other valuable tasks, they produce vitamins that are absorbed into your blood. Water and salts are absorbed from this material and, finally, the more solid remains move into the rectum, ready for elimination.

Far more than just a biochemical process, digestion is highly influenced by our emotional state. Emotions cause cells from the brain's limbic system to release neuropeptides into the bloodstream. Within the blink of an eye, every cell in the body responds to that emotion. Positive thoughts and feelings induce healthy physiological reactions, whereas negative ones create detrimental shifts; these changes are especially noticeable and measurable in our digestive system. Preparing our food with love and eating with gratitude makes a genuine difference to the way our food is digested.

In the past few years, the link between the microorganisms that live in our gut and human health has become more apparent. The gut is sterile up until we leave the womb. As a baby passes through the birth canal, a host of beneficial bacterial microorganisms enter into the baby through its mouth. From there, they make their way through the stomach into the small intestine and finally the large intestine, where they establish themselves in large colonies. Mother's milk contains just the right ingredients to nourish these bacteria and help them flourish. Babies born by C-section will be exposed to different bacteria, picking up their first microbes from the skin of other people and the environment, and formula-fed babies attract different species of bacteria compared to breastfed babies. A balanced microbial community supports digestive health and shapes the very beginning of our immune system.

Recent research has shown that the gut microbiota play a role in nutrient metabolism and energy balance, providing an additional metabolic capacity to extract energy from our diet. The implication of this research is that the gut microbiota are closely associated with several diseases, including obesity and diabetes.

The gut microbiota are important to healthy brain development. In particular, microbiota seem to influence the development of the brain regions involved in our response to stress, along with anxiety, depression and a range of different behavioural patterns. The gut-brain axis is now a major area of research within neuroscience. Microbiota in our gut, sometimes referred to as the 'second genome' or the 'second brain', influence our mood in ways we are only just beginning to understand. Unlike with inherited genes, it seems possible to reshape this second genome.

Diet is known to be a major factor influencing the composition of the gut microbiota. When at Harvard University, microbiologist Peter Turnbaugh found that an extreme diet of meat and cheese caused changes in the kinds of bacteria in the gut, increasing the species *Bilophila wadsworthia* – which is associated with cardiovascular disease – almost immediately.

Traditionally, fermented foods, which have been major contributors to the human diet since early times, have the microbes lactobacillus and bifidobacteria, which is a species known to act positively on the microbiota profile.

It is not only the diet that affects the composition of the gut microbiota: bacterial infections, antibiotic treatment and lifestyle in general can all upset the balance. There is no doubt, however, that the key to ensuring proper digestive function is establishing and maintaining a healthy gut microbiota, and pivotal to health and vitality is good digestion.

conception and birth

From long before conception, the nutrition of those intending to be parents will affect fertility, conception and a baby's development. Sperm takes three months to mature, and women's eggs take one month. Research shows that optimum nutrition before and during pregnancy can have a long-lasting effect on a baby's health. Eating the freshest diet of unprocessed food, grown naturally without the use of chemicals, will help to ensure fertility and boost the chance of conceiving a baby with good physical and mental health.

The potential for life begins when one very small egg cell is penetrated by an even tinier sperm cell. Within four weeks, the egg cell has grown to 10,000 times its original size and turned into an embryo; by the 25th day the heart begins to beat; in the second month the foetus already has eyes, a nose, ears, a mouth and a tongue, and at this stage the brain is growing more quickly than any other organ.

Fats make up 60% of the brain, and two long-chain fatty acids from the omega-3 family – **eicosapentaenoic acid (EPA) and docosahexaenoic acid (DHA)** – are critical for the developing brain. Research shows these long-chain fatty acids are essential in creating the normal structure and function of the brain, and omega-3 deficiencies may lead to reduced visual, motor and cognitive development and mental health conditions.

The EPA and DHA health benefits are linked predominantly to fish that directly supply these essential fatty acids and not the plant-based **alpha-linolenic acid (ALA)**, which the body converts into these longer-chained fatty acids. ALA is generally converted into EPA and DHA in your body at a very low ratio, but some people have a greater ability than others to convert ALA into its long-chain derivatives. There is evidence that the conversion is significantly better in young women than in men. (The high conversion rates reported in young women could be nature's way of preparing for the increased needs of pregnancy and lactation.) Although conversion is slow and incomplete, it does appear to be sufficient to meet the needs of most healthy people if ALA intake is high enough. The richest sources of ALA are flax seed, hemp seed and walnuts. Dark green leafy vegetables are a source of ALA, but you would need to eat a lot to provide an adequate amount.

You eat for two during pregnancy; however, this is not about quantity but quality – good food that nourishes the mother whilst supporting the baby's growth and development. The food a woman eats during pregnancy will have a long-term effect on a growing child and indeed on health throughout life.

Nine months after conception, a baby is born and a single cell has become a human being with consciousness. A newborn baby placed on its mother will move towards the breast and search for the nipple. Colostrum, the first substance suckled from the breast, contains the right nutrients for a baby's needs. This elixir contains more than 700 different bacteria which are essential to the formation of the right composition of the gut microbiota in newborns and are vital in the development of a baby's immune system.

'The richest sources of ALA are flax seed, hemp seed and walnuts. Dark green leafy vegetables are a source of ALA, but you would need to eat a lot to provide an adequate amount.'

As babies become older, the bacterial species present in milk alter, along with the nutritional content, to meet the ever-changing needs of the growing infant. Breast milk is the best way of supporting a baby's developing immune system, providing natural protection against allergies and infection. Research has shown that breastfeeding also reduces a baby's risk for childhood leukaemia, obesity, type 2 diabetes and sudden infant death syndrome. The bond a mother makes with her baby through breastfeeding also provides an irreplaceable feeling of safety, supporting cells to flourish and bringing about optimal development.

It is important to wait for your baby's digestive system to mature and for your baby to be able to chew and swallow before introducing solids. Introducing solids into your baby's diet too early increases the risk of developing food allergies. During the first six months of life, breast milk, or formula if the mother is not breastfeeding, is all the nourishment a baby needs.

As a baby becomes less dependent on the mother for food, the opportunity to share with the wider family increases. All babies develop individual likes and dislikes, but on the whole they have a diversity of tastes and textures that they enjoy. Providing the family is eating wholesome, unprocessed food, there is no need to think about a separate 'baby diet': the baby can simply eat the same food. In the beginning, foods need to be puréed, and certain foods need to be avoided, but before long the youngster will be totally involved in everyday shared eating.

nutrients for conception

All nutrients are important, working in synergy. The following, however, have been studied specifically regarding fertility and conception, and give you an idea of the foods to build your diet around.

Vitamin E	Increased fertility in both men and women has resulted from this powerful antioxidant. Studies show that a low level of Vitamin E in males decreases sperm production. Good levels of this vitamin may also improve sperm motility. In women, Vitamin E helps to normalise hormone production and may improve egg quality.	Food sources: almonds, green leafy vegetables, cold-pressed oils, eggs, hemp seeds, whole grains and avocados.
Vitamin C	Another powerful antioxidant, Vitamin C blocks damaging free radicals. It can increase the count and motility of sperm. It also reduces sperm agglutination, a condition where sperm tend to stick together, which reduces fertility.	Food sources: many fruits, including grapefruit, apples and lemons and vegetables including broccoli, tomatoes, sweet peppers and cabbage.
Vitamin A (as beta-carotene)	Vitamin A helps with the production of cervical mucus. In men, this antioxidant protects sperm from the damaging effect of free radicals. A deficiency is shown to reduce sperm volume and count and increase abnormal sperm.	Food sources: yellow and orange fruits and vegetables, especially carrots, sweet potatoes and dark green leaves.
B Vitamins	For men, Vitamin B12 will help increase the quantity and performance of the sperm. For women, deficiency of Vitamin B6 can result in too much oestrogen in the body. B-Complex vitamins help to reduce stress and maintain a healthy balance of hormones in the body. Folate helps fertility in women and also safeguards the health of an unborn baby (lentils and asparagus are high in folate).	Food sources: beans, nuts, legumes, eggs, meat, fish and whole grains.

Zinc	The focus of numerous studies in fertility of males and females, this nutrient is essential for your pregnancy and your future baby's health. A deficiency of zinc can lead to decreased fertility. It helps women to more effectively use the hormones oestrogen and progesterone to achieve conception. Zinc deficiency is quite common, yet even a mild zinc deficiency can drastically reduce sperm count and affect how long the sperm can live in the vaginal tract.	Food sources: nuts, whole grains, fish, seafood, eggs, pumpkin and sunflower seeds, whole grains, legumes and mushrooms.
Selenium	Another antioxidant, increased levels of selenium have been found to produce higher sperm counts in men. Selenium deficiency causes fragile sperm with easily broken tails. Semen is high in selenium, so it must be replenished regularly. It improves overall reproductive health in women.	Food sources: seafood, tuna, whole grains, asparagus and shiitake.
Magnesium	Magnesium is an essential vitamin which goes hand in hand with the B vitamins. Low levels of magnesium have been linked to miscarriage and infertility.	Food sources: kelp, green vegetables, quinoa, pumpkin seeds, brown rice, beans, rye and buckwheat.
Manganese	The metabolism of the female hormone oestrogen depends on manganese. Therefore, a deficiency of manganese may significantly reduce fertility in women.	Food sources: spinach, chestnuts, oats, rye, beans and nuts.

smoothies for mums to be

Spring green smoothie
Serves 1

175ml carrot juice
50ml nettle juice
large handful sunflower greens
1 avocado, skinned, stoned and chopped
1 teaspoon evening primrose oil
knob of ginger, grated
juice of 1 small lime

Place all the ingredients in
the blender jug and blitz
until smooth.

Summer strawberry smoothie
Serves 1

1 heaped tablespoon flaxseed
10 strawberries
225ml almond milk
1 teaspoon spirulina
½ teaspoon vanilla essence
juice of half a lemon

Blitz the flaxseed to a fine
dust, then add the remaining
ingredients and blitz
until smooth.

Which smoothie maker?

The NutriBullet is incredibly easy to use. It comes with three cup sizes. Add your ingredients to the right sized cup, fix on to the machine, pulse and it's ready in no time at all. It's compact and does not take up a lot of room, and it's easy to clean after use. If you are only going to use it infrequently, this is a very good choice as it is not too expensive.

The all-singing Vitamix is a lot more expensive and there are different models to choose from. It blends quickly and efficiently. It also cooks hot soup from scratch in under five minutes. It's excellent for warming food rather than cooking, thus preserving enzymes and nutrients. It makes a range of ingredients into salsas, dips, ice creams, nut milks and baby purées.

Autumn berry smoothie
Serves 1
100g red grapes
100g blueberries
1 apple, cored and cut into pieces
handful of kale, hard stalks removed
1 tablespoon shelled hemp
1 tablespoon cold-pressed pumpkin oil

Place all the ingredients in
the blender jug and blitz
until smooth.

Winter cacao smoothie
Serves 1
2 heaped teaspoons raw cacao
2 pears, cored and cut into pieces
1 dessert spoon raw almond butter
175ml hemp milk
1 teaspoon spirulina
1 dessert spoon spiced elderberry syrup
(or 1 teaspoon honey)

Place all the ingredients in
the blender jug and blitz
until smooth.

the acid and alkaline balance in the body

The human body works hard at all times to maintain a very delicate pH balance in its fluids, tissues and systems. The term pH means 'potential of hydrogen' and refers to the number of hydrogen ions in a particular solution: this determines the degree of acidity or alkalinity. The pH scale ranges from 0–14. A liquid that has a pH of 7 is neutral, fluids that have a pH below 7 are acidic, and fluids that have a pH above 7 are alkaline.

On the pH scale, each number represents a tenfold difference from adjacent numbers; in other words, a liquid that has a pH of 6 is ten times more acidic than a liquid that has a pH of 7, and a liquid with a pH of 5 is one hundred times more acidic. Coca-Cola has a pH of 2.5. Wheatgrass juice has a pH of 7.4, which is the same as human blood.

An acidic system is a fertile ground for disease. Many experts and health practitioners believe that degenerative disease results from the accumulation of toxins and acid waste in the body. Research has shown that in an acidic environment, normal cells do not thrive and cancer cells flourish. If your blood and cell tissues are too acidic, the naturally acidic cell nucleus and the alkaline cytoplasm which surrounds the cell's nucleus have a diminished bioelectrical potential; this leads to reduced cell vitality and function and, when there is no bioelectrical potential left, the cell dies.

Blood

Most sensitive to an acid–alkaline imbalance is the blood, which needs to be maintained within a pH range of 7.35–7.45. Slightly alkaline blood is essential for cells to function properly. A balanced blood pH is so critical that the body has several self-regulating control mechanisms to protect it from fluctuations.

The body uses the acid-base buffer system to help stabilise pH. When the blood becomes too acidic, buffers are released to return balance. This works conversely if the blood becomes too alkaline, with the release of acidic buffers.

Food

There are two main forces at work in the body that affect the pH – your metabolic activities and the end products of the foods you eat. The metabolic activities that take place every day in your body create acids. As your body generates energy to survive, it will release a number of different acids into your body fluids. When you eat and drink, the end products of digestion and assimilation of nutrients have an acid or alkaline-forming effect. Your choice of food can make a big difference to the acid–alkaline balance and to your health and well-being.

Foods are tested for their alkaline or acid content by burning the food down to its ashes, mixing them with pure water, and testing the solution to see if the ashes are more alkaline or acidic. Sodium, potassium, calcium, magnesium, iron and silicon are alkaline minerals, so if these are the minerals left in the ash, the food is alkaline-forming. If a food contains more acid minerals, such as sulphur, phosphorous, chlorine or iodine, the ash will test acidic and the food is known as acid-forming. From these tests, pH food lists are drawn up. However, there is no single, universal food list for perfect pH, as there are many variables.

The ash residue when food is burnt to test the acid or alkaline content represents complete digestion; however, this is not necessarily automatic in the human body. Our digestive system does not burn food as completely as fire does. When digestion fails to effectively break down our food, the nutrients are not all released and absorbed, which affects alkalinity and acidity.

Many soils, through farming, are depleted of minerals. Use of hybrid crops, pesticides and a cocktail of other chemicals plus artificial fertilisers all affect the composition of food. A food grown far away on an industrial farm, picked unripe and transported thousands of miles before it reaches your kitchen does not have the same composition as local, organically grown, freshly harvested food. Yet pH food lists cannot make a distinction between these differences.

In addition, how food is processed affects pH. Raw milk tends to be more alkaline while pasteurised milk is acid-forming; most cooked grains are acid-forming, whereas sprouted grains are more alkaline.

After metabolism, alkaline-forming foods increase the alkaline reserve in the body, which is essential for creating alkaline buffers. Acids, such as sulphuric or phosphoric acid, remain after acid-forming foods have been metabolised. The body needs to neutralise these before excretion to prevent harming the kidneys or bowel. This is achieved with alkaline-forming minerals such as calcium, magnesium, sodium and potassium. Too much acid-forming food depletes these minerals, all of which have many other important roles in the body – for example, calcium used by the body to maintain the correct alkaline balance is invariably taken from your bones, which leads to a weakening of the bones contributing to osteoporosis.

As within, so without; as without, so within

The Western scientific approach of acid and alkaline aligns to the more spiritual Eastern approach of yin and yang; both concepts carry an equal understanding of balance, which is the key to our health and to the health of the planet. Much human activity creates an imbalance in the environment, contaminating the air we breathe, the water we drink and the food we eat. Changes in the food supply, industrial farming and food processing have created a system that does not harmonise with nature. When the environment is out of balance, so are we.

Industrial development and growth of the chemical industry have spread thousands of toxins throughout the environment.

Deforestation, mining and fracking all cause environmental degradation. Cell phone towers, computers and mobile phones emit electromagnetic waves of varying degrees of chaos. The effect is an 'acidity' in both the outer world of the environment and the inner world of our body. Even though the planet has a self-regulatory system and the human body is constantly striving for balance, this does not imply they can just tolerate whatever happens to them.

<u>Ways to help prevent acidity in the body</u>
In very general terms, sea vegetables, dark green leafy vegetables and freshly picked, ripe, seasonal fruits are alkaline-forming, so it is essential to eat plenty of these.

All refined, processed foods, especially white flour and sugar, are acid-forming. To help maintain an alkaline environment, remove all refined carbohydrate products such as white bread, white rice, pies, pastries, cakes and refined breakfast cereals from your diet.

- Try to eat only naturally grown, organic or biodynamic food.
- If you eat dairy, try to source unpasteurised.
- If you eat meat, limit this to small amounts of the very best quality, organically farmed produce.
- If you eat fish, the best choice would be an oily variety, Marine Stewardship Council approved.
- Severely limit off-the-shelf prepared fruit juices and smoothies – make your own green juices and smoothies.
- Remove all fruits and vegetables picked unripe and shipped from far away.
- Soak all grains, nuts and seeds.
- Start the day with a tablespoon of apple cider vinegar in warm water.
- Minimise caffeine and alcohol, especially beer and spirits.
- If you smoke, give up and avoid other people's smoke.
- Exercise gently each day.
- Get a good night's sleep.

The quality of our thoughts and emotions affects every cell in our body. Positive thoughts and emotions create alkalinity, whilst negative thoughts and emotions are acid-forming.

juicing

Juicing is a brilliant way of harnessing the potent healing power of plant life. Within 20 minutes of drinking a fresh vegetable juice, the nutrients are flowing through you. The absorption rate of nutrients via drinking a juice is higher than eating the whole vegetable. Juices are very easily assimilated; they also give the digestive system, which uses a considerable amount of energy, a rest.

Juices are without a doubt fundamental to a healthy recovery programme from illness. Low-sugar varieties of vegetables containing a large amount of chlorophyll are best, as green juice heals and builds the body. It is best to avoid fruits, as the sugar content can upset blood glucose levels. The addition of lemons and limes to your juice is not a problem, as they are both low in sugar; in addition, they have virtually no fructose, which can be especially disruptive on a healing diet. Lemons and limes are good at counteracting the slightly bitter taste of the dark, green leafy vegetables that provide us with so many nutritional benefits.

If you feel tired or jaded, nutrient-rich, health-enhancing juices help to revitalise your energy. Juices have a cleansing action and help to give your body a kind of spring clean. Once you have a juicer, they are simple to make and delicious to drink. The potent life force in a juice deteriorates very quickly, so drink your juice as soon as it is made. Juices need to be made from organically grown leaves and vegetables and, unless you are avoiding them because of their sweetness, carrot and beetroot along with apples work well with dark green leaves.

Which juicer?

A centrifugal machine is the least effective. The juice extracted from this type of juicer is not of the highest quality as the high-speed spinning that shreds the plant results in rapid oxidation. They are not good at juicing wheatgrass or particularly effective at juicing leafy greens.

A juicer that masticates the plant at a low speed, thus preserving the nutrients, is the best type of juicer. Single auger machines are efficient with dark green leafy vegetables, and there are both vertical and horizontal machines available. Vertical juicers like the Tribest Slowstar produce a good-quality juice and take up a relatively small space on the kitchen side.

Probably the most efficient machines are twin gear juicers like the Greenstar Twin Gear, but they are big and quite expensive. These juicers are capable of juicing all sorts of vegetables, leaves, grasses and fruits, and they can effectively homogenise nuts and seeds for butters. You can also buy quite sturdy stainless steel manual juicers, which are very efficient with grasses and sprouts and generally with most other vegetables. The perfect travelling companion!

what to juice

Alfalfa sprouts	are high in Vitamin K, which is necessary for blood clotting. This is a very important vitamin during pregnancy and childbirth. Alfalfa sprouts are rather strong-tasting on their own, but they blend well with cucumber, celery and carrot.
Cabbage	is an excellent juice for constipation. It is quite a potent juice and may cause wind due to cleansing the intestines. Gently ease yourself into drinking cabbage by blending with carrot and celery. Ginger and lemon are a good addition to take away strong tastes.
Celery	is an especially calming juice, rich in antioxidant and anti-inflammatory nutrients. Celery aids digestion and blends well with apple and spinach.
Cucumber	is a wonderful digestive aid. It is a very cleansing juice and very beneficial to the skin. It is a good juice to blend with the stronger green leaves.
Dandelion	leaves are excellent as part of a spring clean juice; the leaves are diuretic.
Fennel	is very good for indigestion. Fennel, beetroot and carrot juice would make a very good remedy for anaemia. It helps balance hormones and is good for premenstrual and menopausal women.
Garlic	has been used as medicine for thousands of years. It has a beneficial effect on the lymph system, aiding the removal of toxins from the body. Garlic is antibacterial and antiviral, and it's a brilliant self-remedy juice for infections.
Green pepper	is very high in antioxidant Vitamin C, which reduces free radical damage.
Kale	has the highest amount of good-for-you elements amongst green leafy vegetables per calorie of energy. In addition to the wide array of vitamins and minerals, researchers have found 45 antioxidant, anti-inflammatory and anti-cancer nutrients in kale.
Nettle	juice is rich in chlorophyll and minerals, helpful in removing toxins from the blood. Nettles are a natural antihistamine.

Parsley	is a good source of folic acid and Vitamins K, C and A. It is a very potent herb that blends well with other green leaves to make a powerful healing juice.
Purslane	has more omega-3 fatty acids in its leaves than any other land plant. It is a very nutritious green leaf and a mild diuretic.
Sunflower sprouts	are sweet-tasting with a good dose of blood-purifying chlorophyll and tons of vitamins and minerals.
Spinach juice	is an excellent source of Vitamins C and A, along with iron and potassium. It is a good juice for the lymphatic, urinary and digestive systems.
Watercress	is a good juice for intestinal cleansing, but the juice is extremely bitter and needs to be used in combination with other juices.
Wheatgrass	(when grown in rich, vibrant, living soil) can contain all of the known mineral elements and is particularly rich in calcium, magnesium, phosphorous, iron, potassium, sulphur, sodium and zinc.
Beetroot	is a great juice to improve the blood and a good general tonic. The minerals in beetroot juice make it an excellent liver, kidney and gall bladder cleanser. It contains potassium, iron, sodium and manganese and is a good source of silicon.
Carrots	are a good source of antioxidants and the minerals potassium, sodium, calcium and phosphorus, plus iron, magnesium and manganese. The juice helps fight infection and calms the nervous system; it promotes vitality and a sense of well-being. It is an ideal mixer with strong-flavoured green leaves.
Lemon	has a powerful alkaline effect on the body.
Apple	juice is a great cleanser and is a good general all round tonic.

sprouts and sprout greens

Even if you don't have an inch of outdoor space, you can still grow your own nutritious, living food at home. Sprouts and sprout greens are really easy and very inexpensive to grow. All you need for sprouts is a shelf, plus seeds, water, a jar and some mesh; for sprout greens you need a windowsill, seeds, water, a tray and vibrant soil.

All seeds have enzyme inhibitors which the soaking and sprouting process deactivate, making available metabolic and digestive enzymes. Enzymes are the catalysts responsible not only for breaking down food but helping to control all mental and physical processes. Enzymes are essential in transforming chelated minerals into alkaline detoxifiers that neutralise acid cellular waste and prepare them for elimination. Enzymes cannot survive high temperatures; they are destroyed by heat above 43°C and in some cases lower temperatures than this. Too many highly beneficial enzymes are destroyed in our diets of predominantly cooked food.

The increased enzyme activity in soaked and sprouted seeds converts starches into simple sugars, fats into fatty acids and protein into amino acids. By 'pre-digesting' the seed in this way, we make it so much easier for our bodies to make maximum use of the seed's nutrients.

Sprouted seeds are bursting with beneficial nutrition. Sprouting increases Vitamin B content, especially in grains, including B2, B5, and B6. Carotene increases dramatically – sometimes eightfold – and the Vitamin C content of a sprout can be really significant.

Some sprouted seeds can be grown on to produce sprout greens with an abundance of chlorophyll, which is cleansing, anti-inflammatory and rejuvenating. Sprouts and sprout greens are full of vital energy, and when you eat them they can help energise you.

All edible grains, seeds (with the exception of the nightshade family – tomatoes, aubergine, potatoes and peppers) and legumes (with the exception of kidney beans) can be sprouted.

Generally, the following are the best ones to use for sprouting:

- Grains: wheat, kamut, millet, spelt
- Seeds: alfalfa, radish, fenugreek, carrot, sunflower, red clover, buckwheat, quinoa, broccoli
- Legumes: mung, lentils, adzuki beans, peas, chickpeas

The following benefit from soaking before use:

- soak almonds between 12–24 hours
- soak walnuts and hazelnuts 4 hours
- soak hulled pumpkin seeds 12 hours

Seed type	Soak	Sprout
Hulled sunflower	6 hours	2 days
Hulled buckwheat	15 minutes	2–3 days
Wheat/spelt/kamut	8 hours	4 days
Millet	8 hours	24 hours
Quinoa	8 hours	2 days
Mung	12 hours	3–4 days
Chickpeas	12 hours	3–4 days
Green lentils	8 hours	3–4 days
Adzuki bean	12 hours	3–4 days
Alfalfa	6 hours	5 days
Red clover	6 hours	5 days
Fenugreek	6 hours	5 days
Clover	6 hours	5 days
Radish	6 hours	5 days
Broccoli	6 hours	5 days

Sprouting times will vary according to the season and warmth.

How to sprout

Pop a couple of tablespoons of seeds into the sprouting jar and cover generously with filtered water. Screw on a mesh filter lid or fasten a piece of muslin over the top. After soaking for the appropriate time, pour off the soaking water and rinse well. Turn the jar upside down and let it drain. Place the jar on its side in a warm place. Rinse the sprouts in the morning and evening. It is important to keep them moist, warm (room temperature is fine) and well drained until the desired length and age is reached. Once the sprouts are ready, rinse in a colander, wash thoroughly, drain, put in a bowl, cover and store in the fridge.

Sprout greens

Unhulled sunflower, buckwheat and peas grow well as sprout greens.

How to grow sunflower, buckwheat or pea sprout greens

Soak 225g of sunflower, buckwheat or pea seeds for 8 hours, and then rinse well. Fill a seed tray two-thirds of the way with vital organic soil and gently spread the seeds over the soil. Sprinkle with a little extra soil and water well.

Place in a light place but not in direct sunlight; check daily and water as necessary.

They are ready to harvest when there is a mass of shiny green leaves (remove any husks from the sunflower sprouts). Gently cut the sprout greens from the tray and they are ready to enjoy.

Ten reasons to eat sprouts and sprout greens

1. Soaking deactivates enzyme inhibitors, releasing an abundance of enzymes.
2. Proteins, carbohydrates and fats are turned into simple, easy-to-digest compounds.
3. There is a dramatic increase in the vitamin content.
4. Minerals are made easier to assimilate.
5. Phytates and oxalates, which can inhibit the absorption of minerals, are removed.
6. It uses very little energy and so is an environmentally friendly food supply.
7. It connects you intimately to the cycle of life from soil to seed to plant to food to compost.
8. As you are the grower, you can ensure it is chemical free.
9. They are really fresh... because you grew them on the kitchen shelf!
10. They are easy and cheap to grow – plus they are so nutritious, you are satisfied with less.

wheatgrass juice

Benefits of wheatgrass juice
- One of the richest sources of Vitamin A and Vitamin C.
- Contains a balanced range of B Vitamins.
- Good source of calcium, phosphorus and magnesium.
- Contains sodium and potassium in the right balance.
- Provides organic iron, which helps improve blood circulation.
- Can absorb 92 of the known 115 minerals from the soil.
- Highly alkalising.
- 70% chlorophyll, which is cleansing, purifying and restorative. Reduces blood pressure.
- Helps cleanse the liver.
- Relieves constipation.
- Improves blood-sugar problems.
- Neutralises toxins in the body.
- Is gluten free.

Wheatgrass juice may initially cause nausea; this is a reaction to the juice encountering toxins in your system. Barley grass may cause less nausea, but is not as sweet; in fact, it is rather bitter.

How to grow wheatgrass

Materials:
2 x seed trays
organic compost and soil, 50/50
wheat grain

Soak the grain for 12 hours, drain, rinse well and allow to germinate for 12 hours. Keep covered to retain moisture.

Mix the soils together and put into the tray. Moisten the soil so it is damp. Spread the seeds evenly on the tray. Water thoroughly and place in a bright spot. Keep moist. Your wheatgrass will be ready to harvest in 7–10 days.

Once juiced, the wheatgrass should be drunk straight away.

Troubleshooting

- If there is not enough water, the grass will not grow well.
- If there is too much water, the grass will rot.
- If there is not enough light, the grass will be pale and weak.
- If there is too much light (full sunshine), wheatgrass can wilt and dry out.
- If it is too cold, wheatgrass will not grow.
- If it is too hot, wheatgrass will wilt and dry out.
- If it is too hot and humid, the grass will mould and rot.

seven flavours of spring

Radish

This pungent, sweet annual plant from the mustard family is grown for its edible root. There are endless varieties, from the small, sweet crimson radish to the giant, white mooli. Radishes contain Vitamins B and C as well as calcium, copper, iron, magnesium, phosphorous, potassium, sodium and sulphur, plus they are a good source of fibre. Radishes can help remove toxins from the body, which makes them the perfect cleansing spring food.

Nettle

Picking the young shoots of nettles is one of the joys of spring. The leaves are rich in minerals and chlorophyll and have a strong, sweet, peppery zing. Nettles have long been used medicinally, often in cases of iron deficiency (anaemia). They are rich in Vitamin C, which ensures that iron is properly absorbed by the body. An infusion or tincture can be taken to clear uric acid from the system, helping relieve gout and arthritis. Nettles are the perfect ingredient for a spring tonic soup.

Wild garlic

There are a number of different wild garlics; all are easily recognised by their pungent smell. *Alium ursinum*, commonly know as ransoms, are found across Britain and Europe. *Alium tricoccum*, or ramps, are found across North America.

Pungent wild garlic leaves have all the medicinal properties of garlic, with the added benefit of chlorophyll. The shiny green leaves are a perfect cleansing and rejuvenating spring food.

Sorrel

The sour and lemony, pale green leaves of sorrel are some of the first leaves to push their way through the soil each spring. Sorrel is rich in Vitamin C and was traditionally used in the spring to help cleanse the body. The herb contains oxalic acid and should not be used medicinally by those predisposed to arthritis, rheumatism and kidney stones. Oxalic acid is present in abundance in many plant foods, with especially high content in rhubarb, buckwheat, parsley, spinach, beets and cocoa. Small amounts of oxalic acid are generally not harmful.

Asparagus

The perennial vegetable asparagus is loaded with nutrients including folate, Vitamins A, C, E and K, and chromium. It is an effective diuretic because it contains high levels of the amino acid asparagine. It contains inulin, which is beneficial to the digestive tract. Asparagus is a good source of folate, critical for pregnant women as it protects against neural tube defects in babies. Studies have shown that people who have died from Alzheimer's disease had extremely low to no levels of folate.

Lovage

Lovage, a pungent, celery flavoured perennial herb, was grown in the earliest monastic physic gardens. It acts as a digestive, relieves flatulence and has deodorant and antiseptic properties. In the Middle Ages, lovage leaves were laid in the shoes of travellers to keep their feet sweet and fresh. Add fresh leaves to salads and vegetables, and use the seeds in breads and pastries. It also works well with cheese dishes.

Purple sprouting broccoli

Purple sprouting broccoli is a spring highlight, at its best between February and April. The sweet, purple flowering shoots are an absolute storehouse of phytonutrients. It is also packed full of Vitamin C and a good source of iron, folic acid, calcium and Vitamin A. Eat the tender stalks and florets raw or very lightly steamed to preserve the nutrition.

spring health from the meadows and hedgerows

Romy Fraser

I love the start of springtime, when the thin light of the morning comes a little earlier each day, the chorus of birdsong becomes fuller and the first shoots arrive from the cold, wintry soil.

My heart beats faster with the thrill of the newness, something half-remembered, something deep to do with being part of life and nature.

The potent energy from the land emerges from every part of nature that surrounds us. Going for a walk during spring, I feel a sense of awe that I am indeed alive, vibrant, part of this amazing moving world we call Earth and part of this extraordinary process of living that is marked by the seasons.

In the world of freezers, packaged foods and global markets, we no longer need to preserve our foraged foods and garden bounty. In the past we would have stored the autumn harvest through until the following crop. And so we do not generally become as depleted as our ancestors did, nor do we need the restorative nourishment from the first foods of spring in the same way.

However, we do still need to pay attention to the change of temperatures and the reduced sunlight of the winter months. As part of our 21st century ways of living and communicating with one another, we tend to avoid the time to rest during winter and we ignore the time needed to reflect. We push on with our work, and by the time we reach spring, we see there is a pattern of depletion on mental, emotional and spiritual levels as well as physical.

The first foods of spring need little introduction. Nettle (*Urtica dioica*), the champion herb of spring, is a fine tonic, and wild garlic or ransoms (*Allium ursinum*) are naturally mildly antibiotic, but there are others that are potent healers and less often used.

Spring violets (*Viola odorata*) provide a fragrant colour as spring gets going. Traditionally, they're used for coughs (in a syrup), but can also be macerated in a light oil and used for their skin-clearing properties. I love their gentle fragrance. They are beautiful to grow in a shady part of the garden.

Cleavers or goosegrass (*Galium aparine*) is well known amongst children for the way it sticks to clothing (best thrown when no one is looking!). This plant is often the first sign of spring: growing alongside the nettle, it makes a wonderful, cleansing drink, either as a tea or, as Christopher Hedley recommends, by putting a handful in a water jug. Keep topped up with water and drink freely. Your skin will be rejuvenated and your beauty will shine!

I love the hedgerows turning white with hawthorn blossom (*Crataegus oxyacantha and monogyna*), although the time to harvest is just before flowering, when the leaves are still bright, luminous green. Use in salads or as a tea – hawthorn is wonderfully balancing for irregular heartbeats and poor circulation. Don't use if you are taking medication, but it can help as a skin tonic if used externally. It is a herb steeped in history and stories. If you forget to use the flowers for making wine, wait for the berries in autumn. The best way of taking it as a medicine through the winter months is a daily small glass of wine to keep the heart going strongly!

Dandelion (*Taraxacum officinale*) leaves are a food of health. Found on stalls of every Mediterranean market in spring, this delicious tonic salad leaf stimulates the appetite and cleanses the blood. It's not called *pissenlit* (wet the bed) in French for nothing – it is a known diuretic. Dandelion can be used as a mineral-rich spring tonic herb in tea or, alternatively, use the roots roasted as a 'coffee', turn the flowers into wine or just add the leaves to your dish of spring greens.

At Trill Farm, the cowslips (*Primula veris*) herald spring colours with their yellow clusters of bell-like flowers. Delicate and precious, they are found along the old rail track, unlike their cousin the primrose which is found everywhere, covering the banks, meadows and in the sunny gaps amongst the trees in the woodlands. Both plants have often been used for treating coughs and chest complaints – one of Dragana Vilinac's favourite remedies, taught by her third-generation herbalist father in Croatia. I too have learned to love these springtime flowers.

Yarrow (*Achillea millefolium*) pushes up through the lawn grass with strong, dark green feathery leaves. It was known in the days of sword battles as the best wound herb and still today it can be a great internal or external healer. Eat the leaves in spring salads or drink as a tea for fevers. A popular combination is yarrow, elderflower and peppermint – it helps colds and flu, and it is a great remedy for those who suffer from the pollen of summer flowers and grasses.

These are just a few of the plants we can use and I've only

mentioned a few of their delights and properties. There are so many spring plants to cultivate easily or wild harvest. They enrich our lives and, as we become more familiar with them and experience them, so the countryside opens up its secrets and we are invited into a new world, one of stories, folklore and science, history and customs – centuries of intimate connections with the secrets of nature.

Nature is only hidden because we have not been taught the art of observation. It is a world language waiting to be learned and loved. I believe that through plants we can heal ourselves, our stresses and imbalances and our environment. Plants can show us so much more about living and our connection to the world around us, revealing lifetimes of discovery and enjoyment.

Romy Fraser has been at the forefront of using natural remedies for wellbeing since the 1980s. She owns Trill Farm in Devon, a diverse farm that encourages people to connect with the land and develop a deeper understanding of nature.

spring recipes

Radish, carrot, nettle and lemon juice
Wheatgrass, celery and ginger juice
Rhubarb and hemp smoothie
Kefir Ⓓ
Poached rhubarb
Sprouted seed salad Ⓝ Ⓢ
Buckwheat crackers Ⓝ Ⓢ
Spring salad Ⓔ
Beetroot soup with fermented vegetables Ⓓ
Green soup
Quinoa with spring herbs and asparagus Ⓓ
Sorrel frittata Ⓓ Ⓔ
Nettle and spirulina lasagne Ⓖ Ⓓ
Wild garlic grissini Ⓖ
Spring tonic tart Ⓖ Ⓓ
Lemon geranium cake Ⓓ Ⓔ Ⓝ
Gorse flower wine
Spring tonic vinegar
Beech leaf noyau

Ⓖ *– contains gluten*
Ⓓ *– contains dairy*
Ⓢ *– contains soya*
Ⓔ *– contains egg*
Ⓝ *– contains nuts*

Radish, carrot, nettle and lemon juice

serves 1
2 carrots, scrubbed
6 radishes
2 slices lemon
handful of nettles

Cut the carrots, plus the radishes and lemon if necessary, into pieces that will fit the funnel of the juicing machine. Feed in the nettles, then lemons, radishes and carrots. Drink at once.

....

Wheatgrass, celery and ginger juice

serves 1
1 large handful of wheatgrass
5 celery sticks
1 piece ginger

Feed the wheatgrass, then the celery and ginger through the juicer. Drink at once.

....

Rhubarb and hemp smoothie

serves 1 generously or 2 smaller glasses
165g kefir
2 tablespoons shelled hemp seeds
110g poached rhubarb
a thumb-sized piece of ginger, grated

Combine the kefir, hemp, rhubarb and ginger in a blender and blend until smooth. Pour into a glass and serve.

Kefir ⓓ

Milk kefir grains are live, active cultures consisting of yeast and bacteria existing in a symbiotic relationship. They grow and flourish very easily; you should be able to find someone who is happy to share theirs with you, or you can buy them on the internet.

When you receive your grains, pop about 10ml into a clean lass jar and pour in enough organic (ideally raw) milk to cover. After 12 hours, add another 250ml of milk and loosely cover the jar with muslin, then leave for 12–24 hours, stirring the mixture occasionally with a wooden spoon so that the grains can eat the surrounding milk.

When the kefir is ready (you're aiming for thick, sour-tasting yoghurt) strain through a non-metal sieve and collect the grains, or alternatively you can take the grains out with a wooden spoon. If you are not going to repeat the process, put the grains in a jar, pour in milk until just covered and store in the fridge. If you are going to repeat the process, you can increase the quantity of milk to 350ml.

Store your kefir in the fridge. After some time in the fridge, the kefir becomes creamier in texture. If looked after correctly, the kefir grains will grow, probably doubling in size within a few weeks, so you, in turn, will be able to share them.

If you prefer to avoid dairy, repeat the above process using almond milk made at a ratio of 1 part almonds to 4 parts water. If your grains are not happy making almond kefir, you can try making it with a dairy-free probiotic. Use a probiotic capsule or ¼ teaspoon probiotic powder for every 450ml of almond milk and make as above.

....

Poached rhubarb

Makes enough rhubarb for two generous rhubarb and hemp smoothies
225g rhubarb
1 teaspoon honey
juice and zest of 1 orange

Set the oven to 180°C/350°F/Gas mark 4.

Clean the rhubarb and cut into 2 1/2 cm chunks. Place, together with the honey, orange zest and juice, in an ovenproof pot with a lid. Bake until soft – about 15 minutes.

Sprouted seed salad NS

Serves 6
big handful of sprouted sunflower seeds
big handful of sprouted lentils
handful of sprouted alfalfa
handful of sprouted broccoli
3 sun-dried tomatoes, finely shredded
12 almonds, soaked and finely sliced
½ teaspoon fennel seeds
1 clove garlic, crushed
2 teaspoons fresh ginger
2 teaspoons tamari
2 tablespoons olive oil

In a bowl, combine all the sprouted seeds, sun-dried tomatoes and
almonds. Whisk the remaining ingredients together, and gently
mix into the sprouted seed mixture. Serve in bowls with buckwheat
crackers.

....

Buckwheat crackers NS

Makes about 25 thin wedges
225g buckwheat sprouts
55g ground flax
3 tablespoons water
85g walnuts, very finely chopped
2 tablespoons shelled hemp seeds
1 tablespoon miso paste

Whizz the buckwheat sprouts and flax in a food processor, adding
water as necessary to make a firm but slightly sticky mix. Pulse in
the remaining ingredients. Spread the mixture on baking paper to
a thickness of about 3–5mm thick. Dehydrate at 46°C (115°F) for
about 4 hours, before flipping over, peeling off the paper and cutting
the large cracker into neat wedges. Dry for a further 3–4 hours
depending on how thick they are and how crisp you like them.
Cool and store in an airtight container, where they will last a couple
of weeks, or serve them immediately while they are still warm.

Spring salad ⓔ

selection of spring leaves – some options are:
    wild garlic, yarrow, primrose, wood
    sorrel, rocket, mizuna, claytonia,
    chervil, dandelion
1 lightly boiled egg per person
sesame seeds (heaped dessert spoon
    per person)
olive oil
lemon juice
primrose and viola flowers
salt and pepper

Arrange a selection of spring leaves on individual plates and nestle a peeled and halved egg on each. Toast the sesame seeds and grind to a rough powder with a little sea salt (1 heaped dessert spoon sesame seeds, ¼ teaspoon sea salt per person). Blend olive oil, lemon juice and black pepper together (1 tablespoon olive oil, 1 teaspoon lemon juice per person). Pour the dressing over the leaves, then scatter over the sesame powder and finally the flowers.

....

Beetroot soup with fermented vegetables ⓓ

Serves 4
50g butter
700g beetroot, peeled and chopped
1 medium onion, peeled and chopped
1 potato, scrubbed or peeled and chopped
1.2 litres vegetable stock
4 tablespoons of fermented vegetables
    (sauerkraut or kimchi)
salt and pepper

Melt the butter in a thick-bottomed pan and stir in the beetroot, onion and potato. Cook gently for 5 minutes. Add the stock and bring to the boil. Simmer gently for 45 minutes. Cool slightly, then sieve or blend until smooth, return to the pan and heat through. Season as you feel necessary with salt and pepper.

Divide between 4 bowls; put a spoonful of fermented vegetable in the middle of each.

Green soup

Serves 4
1 medium floury potato, peeled and diced
6 spring onions, thinly sliced
1 litre vegetable stock
4 handfuls of chickweed
6 leaves sorrel, torn into pieces
small bunch of chervil
small handful of hedge garlic (if you can find
    it; alternatively, a small bunch of
    wild garlic)
4 handfuls of nettles, blanched and
    finely chopped
juice of half a lemon
gorse buds and chervil sprigs
salt and pepper

Put the potato, spring onions and stock into a pan and bring to the
boil; simmer gently for 15 minutes. Add the chickweed and sorrel
and cook for a further 2 minutes. Remove from the heat, cool
slightly, then blend until smooth. Return to the pan.

Roughly chop the chervil and garlic and add to the soup along
with the nettles. Simmer gently for a minute, remove from the heat,
add the lemon juice and season well with salt and freshly ground
black pepper.

Divide between 4 bowls and top with gorse flower buds and
chervil sprigs.

Quinoa with spring herbs and asparagus ⒟

Serves 4
350g asparagus
450ml vegetable stock
2 onions, finely sliced
3 tablespoons olive oil
3 tablespoons water
3 lovage leaves, finely shredded
225g quinoa
1 large handful of herbs (parsley, tarragon,
    chives, chervil, rocket, fennel – whatever
    you have), roughly chopped
25g butter
¼ teaspoon salt
pepper

Break the coarse ends off the asparagus and discard. Cut off the tips and plunge them into boiling water for 1 minute. Strain, (keeping the liquid to use as stock, either in this or another recipe) and refresh the tips in cold water. Set aside. Cut the stalks into 1cm pieces.

Bring the stock to the boil and season with salt and pepper. In a thick-bottomed pan, gently cook the onions in the oil with an equal amount of water. When they have softened and the water has evaporated, add the lovage, asparagus stalks and quinoa, stir well, then pour in the stock and allow to cook for 15 minutes, by which time the quinoa should be cooked and all the liquid absorbed.

Remove from the heat and stir in the asparagus tips, herbs and butter.

Sorrel frittata ⓓⓔ

Serves 4
8 eggs
25g hard sheep's cheese or any favourite
    hard cheese
25g butter
250g sorrel, stalks removed and
    finely shredded
salt and pepper

Preheat the oven to 180°C/350°F/Gas mark 5.

Break the eggs into a bowl, add salt and pepper and whisk well with
a fork. Set aside. Grate the cheese.

Melt the butter in a shallow frying pan, suitable to go in the
oven. Add the sorrel and gently wilt, stirring for 1 minute. Add in the
egg mixture.

Cook over a low heat for a couple of minutes or until the sides
begin to set; pull the sides into the middle and cook for a further
30 seconds. Place the grated cheese on top, transfer to the oven and
cook for 10 minutes or until set and golden.

Nettle and spirulina lasagne ⒼⒹ

Serves 8

For the spirulina pasta dough
110g strong white flour
110g spelt flour, sifted
4 tablespoons water
2 tablespoons olive oil
1 dessert spoon spirulina
pinch of salt

Place the mixed flours onto a working surface in a mound, make a well in the centre and put the water, olive oil, spirulina and salt into the well. Slowly incorporate the flour into the liquid until the mixture resembles a coarse dough. You may have to add a little water at this stage to make the paste pliable enough. On a clean working surface, knead the dough with firm hand movements until it is smooth and silky; it will take about 10 minutes. Put the dough in a clean, lightly oiled bowl, cover with a plate and leave in the fridge for at least half an hour before using.

For the nettle filling
350g nettle tops
50g pine kernels, roughly chopped
50g feta, diced
25g basil, torn
250ml well-flavoured stock

Plunge the nettle tops into boiling water for 30 seconds, drain and refresh in cold water. Strain and press out any excess moisture. Very finely chop the nettles, then add the pine kernels, feta, basil and stock. Mix well together.

For the béchamel
900ml milk
2 bay leaves
1 thick slice of onion
12 peppercorns
75g butter
40g spelt flour

Place the milk in a saucepan with the bay leaves, onion and peppercorns, place over a low heat and bring slowly up to simmering point, which will take around 5 minutes. Remove the saucepan from the heat.

Melt the butter in a pan and add the flour, stirring vigorously to incorporate well and cool slightly. Strain the infused milk, then slowly pour onto the butter and flour mixture, beating well all the time. Bring to the boil and cook gently for 2 minutes. Remove from the heat and cover with wet greaseproof paper to prevent a skin from forming.

For the crumb top
4 cloves garlic, finely chopped
1 onion, finely chopped
2 tablespoons olive oil
50g butter
225g wholemeal breadcrumbs
handful of parsley, finely chopped
1 dessertspoon thyme, chopped
salt and pepper

Cook the garlic and onion in the olive oil for a couple of minutes, then add the butter and allow to melt before stirring in the breadcrumbs and herbs. Season as necessary with salt and black pepper.

To assemble:

Cut the pasta dough in half. Roll each half out thinly and cut into lasagne sheets. Lightly oil the lasagne dish, ladle half the nettle mixture into the dish and cover with lasagne sheets. Repeat with the remaining nettle mixture and lasagne. Spoon over the béchamel sauce, top with the breadcrumbs and bake in the oven until bubbling and golden brown.

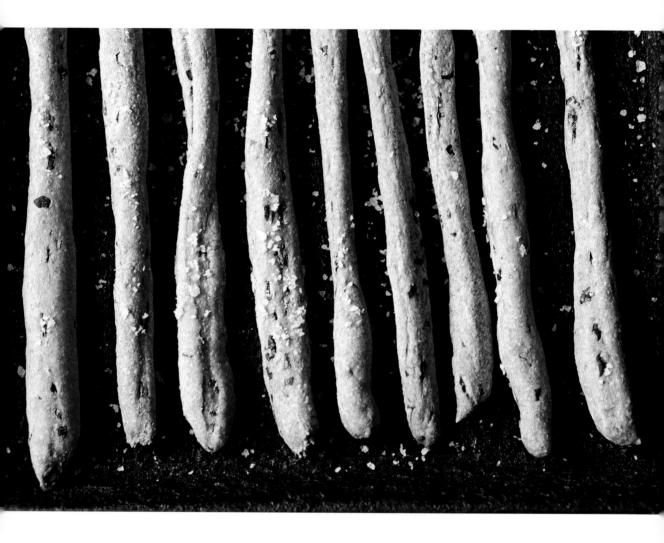

Wild garlic grissini ⓖ

Makes around 15
For the ferment
150g unbleached strong white flour
120ml warm water
20g yeast

For the dough
350g wholemeal bread flour
1 teaspoon sea salt
16 leaves wild garlic, very finely shredded
4 tablespoons olive oil
water to mix

Combine the ingredients for the ferment and leave covered in a warm place for 1 hour.

Combine the dough ingredients in a bowl and stir in the ferment and enough water to make a soft dough, then leave for 10 minutes. Lightly oil a work surface and gently knead the dough for a minute or two. Return to the cleaned and lightly oiled bowl and leave for 10 minutes. Repeat twice, then leave for 1 hour. Heat the oven to 180°C/350°F/Gas mark 4.

Lightly flour a table and roll the dough out into a large rectangle, about 20cm wide. Cut thin strips across the width of the dough, then roll and elongate each strip to 30cm. Place on an oiled baking tray and bake for about half an hour until golden brown, then remove and cool on a rack.

Spring tonic tart ⓖⓓ

Serves 6
175g wholemeal flour
110g porridge oats
110g butter
110g carrot, grated
450g nettle tops
handful each of parsley, chervil and
    chives, chopped
handful of sorrel, finely shredded
3 eggs
275ml oat milk
salt and pepper

Preheat the oven to 180°C/350°F/Gas mark 4.

Whizz the flour, oats and butter in a processor until crumb-like,
then add the grated carrot and continue to process until the mixture
comes together to form a ball. Carefully roll the pastry out, then line
a 25cm loose-bottomed flan tin with it. Chill in the fridge.

Blanch the nettles in hot water and refresh in cold water, then
squeeze dry and chop. Mix with the parsley, chervil, chives and
sorrel. Place in the tart case. Whisk the eggs and milk together with
salt and black pepper and pour over the nettles.

Bake in the oven for 40 minutes, lowering to 170°C/300°F/
Gas mark 3 after 15 minutes. Leave to cool for 10 minutes before
removing from the tin and sliding onto a serving plate.

Lemon geranium cake ⓓⓔⓝ

knob of butter and lemon geranium leaves for
    lining the tin
350g butter
350g rapadura sugar
7 eggs
350g ground almonds
juice and zest of 1 lemon
6 medium lemon geranium leaves, stalks
    removed and finely chopped

Preheat the oven to 180°C/350°F/Gas mark 4.

Lightly butter a 25cm diameter cake tin and line with baking paper, then lightly butter once more and cover the lined and buttered base with geranium leaves.

Place the butter and sugar into a bowl and beat together until they are light and fluffy. Beat in the eggs alternately with the ground almonds, then stir in the lemon juice and zest and finely chopped lemon geranium leaves (or you could put all the ingredients into a bowl of an electric mixer and beat together until light and fluffy).

Carefully spoon the mixture into the prepared tin without disturbing the leaves. Smooth over the top and bake for 35–40 minutes. The cake is done when it is the softer side of firm to a finger touch and slightly shrunk from the edge of the cake tin. Leave the cake for 10 minutes before inverting onto a serving plate. Carefully peel away the baking paper and leave to cool before serving.

....

Gorse flower wine

2.5 litres water
2 litres gorse flowers
large piece of ginger, finely sliced
zest and juice of 2 lemons
650g demerara sugar
1 teaspoon wine yeast

Bring the water to the boil, then allow to cool. Place the flowers in a bowl, pour the cooled water over them, cover with a cloth and leave for a day, stirring occasionally.

Pour into a large pan, add the ginger and lemon zest and bring to the boil. Keep it barely simmering for half an hour, before straining and stirring in the lemon juice and sugar.

Allow to cool, then cream the yeast with some of the liquid and add to the bowl. Cover with a cloth and ferment for 2 days. Pour into a demijohn, fix with an airlock and leave until all fermentation has stopped. Siphon off and bottle. Keep for at least 3 months before drinking.

Spring tonic vinegar

Infusing herbs in apple cider vinegar combines the healing properties of the vinegar with the healing essence and rich mineral content of herbs.

6 yarrow leaves
6 dandelion leaves
small handful of nettles
4 lovage leaves
bunch of chervil
apple cider vinegar (raw)

Put the yarrow leaves and dandelion leaves into a sterilised ½ litre jar. Chop the nettles, lovage and chervil and add to the jar. Pour the apple cider vinegar over the herbs to fill the jar. Cover tightly and allow to extract for 2 weeks in a cool, dark place. After 2 weeks, strain the herbs through cheesecloth, put the strained liquid into a clean bottle and cap tightly.

Take one tablespoon in warm water on rising as a general tonic.

Beech leaf noyau

Beech is the symbol for the wisdom within ancient learning. The leaves are cooling, astringent and antiseptic.

young beech leaves
gin
1 dessert spoon honey for every pint of liquid

Gather young, soft, velvety beech leaves and pack into a jar. Cover with gin and leave to steep for 1 month. Strain, add the honey, mix well, pour into bottles and seal.

summer

dairy

Milk – good or bad?

The ability of a particular food to nourish us depends greatly on the way it has been produced and processed. Organic raw milk from healthy, small herds of grass-fed cows is a very different food from industrially produced milk that has been pasteurised and homogenised; however, do we really need to drink any milk besides our own? Are there any benefits in drinking the milk from another mammal? For a myriad of reasons, many people think that milk from another species should not be part of the human diet, particularly after infancy.

Lactose

Lactose is the sugar found in milk and is actually two sugars – galactose and glucose – bonded together. The enzyme lactase breaks the bond so that the individual sugars can be digested. After the age of four, depending on race and ethnicity, many people (and in some cases most people in a given culture) lose the ability to produce the enzyme lactase. When lactose is not effectively broken down, consuming dairy can provide food for pathogenic bacteria in the gut, leading to bloating and gas. There is much evidence to suggest that people who switch to raw milk do not suffer the same symptoms of lactose intolerance. It is thought that lactase-forming bacteria in raw milk break down the sugar lactose.

Casein and whey

Casein, found in the solid part of milk, and whey, found in the liquid part of milk, are the two common proteins that cause food allergy in young children. Doctors generally think that you can grow out of this allergy, but for many children this is not the case. Casein shares structural similarities to gluten, the protein in grains that

can play havoc with the lining of the intestine. Those who think drinking milk is detrimental to health cite casein as a major cause of leaky gut, and this may well be the case. However, people who are gluten intolerant often develop a dairy intolerance, so it could be that gluten weakens the gut lining and, once the problem is created, casein begins to slip through the intestinal wall and create a reaction. Casein in any case is a hard-to-digest protein that can create mucus on the intestinal wall, which then inhibits absorption of nutrients and encourages the growth of the wrong bacteria.

Calcium

Our physiology requires a ratio of about 2:1 calcium to magnesium. In dairy products the ratio is 10:1. Foods with a far better calcium to magnesium ratio are green vegetables, especially broccoli, kale, turnip tops, dandelion and watercress, as well as sea vegetables, nuts and seeds. Pasteurised milk acidifies the body pH, and the alkalising mineral calcium is predominantly used to neutralise the acid. Countries with the highest consumption of pasteurised dairy products have the highest incidences of osteoporosis.

Whole milk

Whole cows' milk contains up to 5% fat per 100ml and is more nutritious than semi-skimmed and skimmed milk as it is the fat element that contains Vitamins A, D, E and K; they are important, among a myriad of other things, for keeping bones healthy. By removing the fat, we upset the natural synergy of the nutrients in milk.

Homogenisation

Homogenisation uses pressure to force milk through small holes to break up the fat globules. The process creates such tiny globules that they remain suspended evenly in the milk, producing a uniform consistency. It also gives milk a longer shelf life. There is a theory that this process contributes to heart disease, diabetes and allergies. This is due largely to the homogenisation process boosting the absorbability of the enzyme xanthine oxidase through the intestinal wall and into the blood stream.

Pasteurisation

The process of pasteurisation involves heating milk to 71.7°C for at least 15 seconds and no more than 25 seconds. Once the milk has been heated, it is then cooled very quickly to less than 3°C. It is a process used to destroy dangerous bacteria, but pasteurisation does more than this – it also kills off harmless and useful bacteria and destroys some nutritious constituents.

Pasteurisation destroys the ability of certain proteins in milk to bind the important vitamin folate and hence help its absorption. Heat treatment might also cause a similar inactivation of other protein carriers, for example those for zinc and Vitamin B12. 25% or more of the Vitamin C content is lost and there is about a 10% loss of Vitamins B1, B6 and B12. Pasteurisation distorts the fragile milk protein into different shapes or configurations, much of which has been found to be allergenic.

Organic vs. non-organic
Cows are natural herbivores and pasture-fed animals produce a higher quality food than those who live in confined dairy operations and are fed grain. When large numbers of cows are kept in small spaces under stressful conditions they often become ill and are then treated with drugs. Organic pasture-fed cows support, through depositing dung, healthy fertile soil, and by eating a natural diet, they produce milk higher in Vitamin E, beta carotene and the antioxidants lutein and zeaxanthin than cows reared inside on grain. In addition there are higher levels of omega-3 essential fatty acids.

Environment
A closed farm system, such as biodynamic, means that the farm does not keep animals that the farm is not able to support. This means that dairy cows graze on grass for much of the year and are not fed food from outside the farm. Intensively farmed dairy cows rely on imports of grain and soya from overseas, increasing demand for land in other countries and adding to greenhouse gas emissions from change of land use overseas. Small herds of cows living on well-managed pastures decrease soil erosion, increase soil fertility and improve water quality because less manure and urine is generated. All cows emit methane, which is a greenhouse gas more powerful than carbon dioxide. The amount of methane a cow emits will depend on the breed and the food it eats.

Breed of cow
Cows' milk contains different types of protein – including ones called A1 and A2 depending on the cow's genetics. All cows used to be A2 cows until a naturally occurring genetic mutation in European cows changed the genetics of milk-producing cow herds.

These two proteins digest quite differently from each other. Some people simply react to the A1 protein and, if they drink milk from an alternative A2 breed, the problem goes away. A1 breeds include Holstein and Rhodesian and A2 breeds are the older breeds of cows such as Jerseys, Guernseys, Asian and African cows.

Raw milk

Raw milk tends to be produced on farms with small herds grazing on pasture and can be bought from the farm gate, farmers' markets and even online. The Food Standards Agency warns that it 'could be harmful' and should be avoided by the young, elderly, pregnant or unwell. By law, unpasteurised milk from cows, goats or sheep must carry a warning: 'This milk has not been heat-treated and may therefore contain organisms harmful to health.' The greatest concern is TB, but no one has caught TB from drinking milk in the last 50 years, as the health tests on all milking cows are very rigorous. The percentage of raw milk to total milk on the market is very small, and the total organically produced raw even less.

One of the major advantages of drinking raw, organic milk is that it contains enzymes that perform an amazing array of tasks, along with beneficial bacteria that enhance immunity, digestion and nutrient assimilation. Many of the enzymes and bacteria are destroyed when the milk undergoes pasteurisation.

Fermentation

Fermented milk products are easier to digest. This is because the fermentation process breaks down the milk sugar lactose into single sugars and the hard-to-digest proteins into amino acids. In addition, it makes minerals and vitamins more bio-available and provides beneficial lactic bacteria. It's easy to make kefir or yoghurt at home and, if you are unable to source raw milk, the transformative wonder of fermentation can even help to rejuvenate the life force and nutritional value of pasteurised milk – making sure, of course, the milk is organic.

Another traditional milk ferment is cheese. There are many artisan cheesemakers producing a variety of flavours and textures from unpasteurised milk. If you are going to eat cheese, search out these artisan cheesemakers who supply independent shops and sell at farmers' markets.

Weigh up the pros and cons for yourself of drinking milk. On an energetic level, does drinking the milk of another species feel right? Listen to your body; how well do you digest dairy? If it feels good for you, source the most natural milk you can – raw milk from an organic or biodynamic dairy farmer is by far the best, both ethically and nutritionally.

Milk alternatives

Plant-based milk alternatives are obviously free from animal welfare issues and, as they are plants, absorb carbon, but they are not without their problems: the demand for soya and almonds has caused a serious environmental impact in the USA and South America, so if you choose to include soya or almond in your diet, be sure you know their provenance. It's easy to grow oats in the UK and it would be possible to successfully grow quinoa and hemp as well as soya beans, but ready made milks generally use imported ingredients. The three easiest milks to make yourself are almond, oat and hemp.

Almond milk

Almond milk is sweet, nutty and nutritious and a good source of magnesium, calcium and Vitamin E, though obviously not suitable for those with nut allergies. California supplies 84% of the world's almonds. The trees require huge quantities of water year round in this very dry state. In addition, this vast monoculture requires in excess of 1.5 million colonies of bees to be transported in to pollinate the trees, resulting in massive bee losses. Ecomil brand almond milk is made from organic almonds from Spain.

Oat milk

Oat milk is a good source of Vitamin E and folic acid, with high levels of phytonutrients. A very easy milk to make yourself from UK oats, simply soak oats overnight in a ratio of 1 part oats to 3 parts water and whizz together the next morning – strain through muslin or use as it is. It will keep in a Kilner jar in the fridge for several days.

Hemp milk

Hemp makes a creamy textured milk which is packed full of nutrients, including easy to assimilate protein, omega-3 and 6 fatty acids in the right ratio for human nutrition, and a wide range of minerals and vitamins.

Coconut milk

Coconut milk has a very creamy texture, but the flavour for some people can be a bit overwhelming. Coconut milk is high in fat, mostly in the form of medium-chain saturated fatty acids. 50% of this fat content is lauric acid, which is also found in human milk and is known to have antiviral and antibacterial properties. The fat content in coconut milk is quickly turned into energy.

Hazelnut milk

Hazelnut milk has a stronger, nuttier flavour than almond milk and is rich in alpha-linolenic acid, folic acid and Vitamin E. Wild-gather cobnuts in the autumn and make your own milk from the soft, fresh nut.

Quinoa milk

Quinoa milk has a nutty flavour. It is a complete protein and a very good source of iron and calcium. Quinoa from South America potentially carries both a high environmental and social cost. UK-grown quinoa is now available.

Rice milk

Many people consider this the best option if you have a dairy, nut or soya allergy. It lacks protein, Vitamin A and the fats found in other milks, and it is also rather high in sugar.

Soya milk

Many people who are allergic to milk are also allergic to soya. Soya is in fact one of the eight allergens that cause 90% of allergic reactions. Soya contains protease inhibitors which interfere with digestive enzymes, leading to poor protein digestion and an overworked pancreas. Fermented soya products are far easier to digest than soya milk. For more information on soya, see Diane Osgood on page 134.

good and bad fats

How important are fats in your diet? Which fats are health-giving? Which fats are safe to cook with? Should you minimise saturated fat and cholesterol for a healthy heart? Does fat make you fat? For the last sixty years, there has been an endless stream of changing information about dietary fat, leading to a great deal of confusion.

For decades we were told that a low-fat diet was the best way to lose weight and prevent or control heart disease along with a variety of other conditions. The crusade against dietary fat was originally based on the flawed work of Ancel Keys. His research led to the public message that dietary fat must be minimised and replaced with grains and that saturated fat should be replaced by unsaturated fat. The unfortunate result was a vast range of low-fat and fat-free foods filling the grocery shelves, generally compensating for their lack of flavour with the addition of salt and sugar. Low-fat and high carbs became the nutritional mantra, but heart disease was not controlled and the weight did not fall off. Fat needed rethinking.

Natural, unprocessed fats all have specific roles in the body. To fully appreciate these roles, it is worth understanding the chemical nature of a fat.

A molecule of any solid or liquid fat is made up of fatty acids. All fatty acids are made up of a carbon chain to which hydrogen is attached. Fatty acids have three basic purposes in your body: provide energy, provide the building blocks for all cell membranes and provide the raw materials that can be converted into other substances that perform very particular functions in the body such as hormones. There are three types of fatty acids found in fats: saturated, monounsaturated and polyunsaturated.

Saturated fats
Saturated fats are so called because the carbon atoms in the chain carry the maximum number of hydrogen atoms possible and are thus saturated with them. They are predominantly found in the fat cells of animals and tropical fats. They come in three different chain lengths.

Short-chained saturated fatty acids of up to eight-carbon length are used mainly to produce energy. They are easy to digest and are good for people with weak digestion. Medium-chained saturated fatty acids are also used by the body for energy production. Long-chained saturated fatty acids are harder to digest, less easily burned as fuel and are more readily stored as fat.

Monounsaturated fats

A **monounsaturated fat** has one double bond in the carbon chain and is slightly less stable than a **saturated fat**. It is found in avocados, olives and nuts. Oleic acid, present in olive oil, is a **monounsaturated fat** that is known to have a beneficial effect on health. The many benefits include improving the function of the heart and circulatory system, helping to optimise the way the brain works and boosting memory power.

Polyunsaturated fats

These fats contain more than one double bond; because of these weak links they are the fats most susceptible to damage.

The body can synthesise most of the fats it needs from your diet. However, there are two polyunsaturated fatty acids, **alpha-linolenic acid (ALA)** and **linoleic acid (LA)**, that the body is unable to synthesise, so these essential fatty acids must be obtained from food. These two essential fats are used to build omega-3 and omega-6 derivatives, which are important in the normal functioning of all tissues of the body. Omega-3 derivatives **eicosapentaenoic acid (EPA)** and **docosahexaenoic acid (DHA)** and omega-6 derivative **arachidonic acid (AA)** are precursors of prostaglandins.

Prostaglandins are short-lived, hormone-like chemicals that regulate a whole range of cellular activities. One of the many roles of prostaglandins is controlling inflammation. Prostaglandins formed from omega-3s are anti-inflammatory, but the ones formed by omega-6 are inflammatory. For this reason, the right ratio of omega-6 to omega-3 in the diet is obviously very important. A ratio of 3 parts omega-6 to 1 part omega-3 is considered the right balance; however, our Western diet in recent years has leaned heavily on consumption of omega-6 vegetable oils like soya and corn, making the ratio closer to 24:1. This can be seen as one of the contributory factors to degenerative inflammatory diseases.

To be able to fulfil their roles in the body, fats need to be as natural as possible and not over-processed. During the 1950s, hydrogenation was introduced into the food industry, based on the belief that polyunsaturated vegetable oils were superior to saturated fats. For the food industry, hydrogenated fats had a major economic advantage over natural saturated fats – they were cheaper. Using a chemical process, hydrogenation forces the addition of hydrogen onto the carbon chain of a polyunsaturated fatty acid. We now know that these fats are not better for our health.

The chemical structure of an artificially hardened fat is quite different from that of a naturally saturated fat. A very slight change – the rotation of the molecule around a double bond – twists a fatty acid from its natural cis configuration into an unnatural trans configuration, creating a trans fatty acid. This slight change drastically changes its properties, its performance in our body and its effects on our health.

Trans fats are found predominantly in processed foods, including pastries, cakes and deep-fried products. The level of trans fats in processed foods has dropped dramatically since accepting how harmful they are. Small amounts of naturally occurring trans fats are found in some meat and dairy products, though there has been little research into their effect on human health.

Over the last few years, experts have begun to challenge the science that demonised saturated fat. Recent studies have failed to show a link between saturated fat intake and risk of cardiovascular disease; in fact, saturated fat has been found to be protective. Scientific evidence is proving that refined carbohydrates and sugar in particular are the real culprits of cardiovascular disease. Fats are essential to life, so the best quality fats from all groups should form part of a balanced diet.

Food choices

Saturated fat

Saturated fats are very stable, which means they are the best fats to use when cooking. **Butter** is a good source of saturated fat and this, if you eat animal foods, is a good traditional saturated fat choice in the UK. The butter must come from grass-fed cows, not animals raised primarily on an unnatural diet for the species. Organically reared cows living in their natural environment, accumulating minimal toxins in their fat, produce a far healthier butter. Often, but not necessarily, clarifying helps the dairy intolerant by removing the milk proteins.

From the tropics there is **coconut oil**, which is solid at room temperature. It is a stable oil, which makes it very suitable to cook with. Coconut oil contains a number of beneficial fatty acids including lauric acid, which converts in the body into monolaurin, which destroys harmful fungus, bacteria and viruses.

Monounsaturated fats

Olive oil is the best-known monounsaturated fat. It contains around 75% oleic acid, which is reasonably resistant to heating. Damage-prone polyunsaturated fats make up only about 11% of olive oil. To protect the oil from damage, add an equal amount of water to the oil before cooking. Use olive oil liberally in dressings.

'The so-called "bad" type of cholesterol, LDL, is specifically sent to the wound by the liver and this is why patients with heart disease are seen to have high levels in their body. Unfortunately, because LDL is found at the "crime scene", the cholesterol is mistakenly blamed for the heart condition when in fact it is nature's way of trying to combat it.' – Natasha Campbell-McBride

Polyunsaturated fats

Polyunsaturated fats are the least stable and not suitable for cooking with. Heating polyunsaturated oils creates free radicals, together with various breakdown products, all of which are harmful to health. The two essential polyunsaturated fats are **linoleic acid (omega-6)** found in **safflower**, **sunflower** and **pumpkin seeds** and **alpha-linolenic acid (omega-3)** found in **flax**, walnut and **dark green leaves.** From these essential fatty acids, superunsaturated derivatives are made. A healthy body is able to make all the necessary conversions, but the derivatives of these essential fatty acids can also be obtained from food.

Important derivatives of linoleic acid are **gamma linolenic acid (GLA)**, which is found in **hemp oil** and **evening primrose oil,** and **arachidonic acid (AA)**, which can be found in **eggs** and **dairy** produce. Derivatives of alpha-linolenic acid are stearidonic acid **(SDA)** found in **blackcurrant seed oil** and **spirulina**, together with **eicosapentaenoic acid (EPA)** and **docosahexaenoic acid (DHA)**, which are found in the oils of **cold-water fish** and **algae.**

As plant-based oils are vulnerable to light, heat and oxygen, they should be protected at every stage of production. When choosing polyunsaturated oils, make sure they are cold-pressed, unrefined and in dark glass bottles.

Cholesterol

Cholesterol is not a fat but rather a soft, waxy, fat-like substance that circulates in the bloodstream. It is absolutely vital to life as every cell in the body uses cholesterol – it is essential for reproduction, the immune system, cell communication, Vitamin D production and brain function. In fact, the brain itself is 25% cholesterol.

Cholesterol cannot dissolve in the blood, so your liver combines it with special proteins called lipoproteins to 'liquefy' it. The lipoproteins used by the liver are **very low-density lipoproteins (VLDL)** – these are metabolised in the blood to produce **low-density lipoproteins (LDL)** or **high-density lipoproteins (HDL)**. The liver is responsible for over 80% of your cholesterol level. LDL is transported away from the liver and HDL is transported back to the liver.

Many doctors, researchers and scientists are challenging our perception of cholesterol as 'foe'. The most comprehensive review of all available science on cholesterol and heart disease has been undertaken by Dr Uffe Ravnskov, who has written extensively on the subject and from a lifelong study has concluded there is no evidence that too much animal fat and cholesterol in the diet promotes atherosclerosis or heart attacks; he believes that low-cholesterol diets and cholesterol-lowering drugs are wrong. The research of Dr Fred Kummerow over the past 60 years has repeatedly demonstrated that there is no correlation between high cholesterol and the plaque formation that leads to heart disease.

So what's going on?

An alternative theory to atherosclerosis is built around arterial damage. When our arterial walls are damaged and there is inflammation, our bodies set out to heal the damaged site. They do this by creating the repair cement we know as plaque from cholesterol, calcium and fibrin to repair the damage before the arterial wall develops a leak and we begin to bleed internally. Cholesterol is, in fact, a healing agent. Cholesterol travels from the liver to the wound in the form of LDL. When the wound heals and the cholesterol is removed, it travels back to the liver in the form of HDL cholesterol.

Nutritionist Natasha Campbell-McBride, who has researched the diet–heart hypothesis, believes we have clearly misunderstood the role of cholesterol:

'The so-called "bad" type of cholesterol, LDL, is specifically sent to the wound by the liver and this is why patients with heart disease are seen to have high levels in their body. Unfortunately, because LDL is found at the "crime scene", the cholesterol is mistakenly blamed for the heart condition when in fact it is nature's way of trying to combat it.'

Rather than being the cause of plaque build-up, cholesterol is a healing agent for sites that are damaged with inflammation. If arterial inflammation, not cholesterol, is the problem, we need a whole new approach to heart disease.

what causes arterial wall damage?	action
trans fatty acids	only eat natural fats
too much omega-6 fatty acid in the diet, which promotes inflammation	balance omega-6 with omega-3; a good ratio is 3:1 and a good food is hemp seed
diets high in acid-forming foods	limit acid-forming foods and eat plenty of alkalising foods like green leafy vegetables
high homocysteine levels	ensure plenty of folic acid, B12 and B6 in the diet
agricultural chemicals	eat organic food
processed food, especially white grains and sugar, which contribute to inflammation	eat freshly prepared whole foods and reduce carbohydrate and grain consumption
industrial chemicals	avoid as much as possible
stress	minimise stress by adopting relaxation techniques, be it yoga, singing or dancing

sugar

<u>Sugar classifications</u>

Sugars fall into four main categories: these are monosaccharides, disaccharides, oligosaccharides and polysaccharides.

Monosaccharides are simple, single molecule sugars, and the most common monosaccharide is *glucose* – 'blood sugar' – which is the immediate source of energy for our cells. Monosaccharides are the basic structure that all carbohydrates are reduced to for use in the body; they include *fructose*, which is known as fruit sugar, and *galactose*, which is present in mammals' milk.

Disaccharides are two molecules joined together:

Sucrose is made up of a 1:1 ratio of fructose and glucose. It is found in sugar cane and sugar beets.

Maltose is made up of two glucose molecules and is usually formed by the germination of grains.

Lactose is made up of galactose and glucose.

There are three types of oligosaccharides. These sugars are important in supporting the health of the gut microbiota. Generally oligosaccharides are only partially digested in the human gut – the undigested part provides food for beneficial bacteria.

Fructo-oligosaccharides (FOS) consist of short chains of fructose molecules.

Galacto-oligosaccharides (GOS) consist of short chains of galactose molecules.

Mannan-oligosaccharides (MOS) are composed of two sugars, mannose and glucose.

Oligosaccharides are generally not more than ten monosaccharide molecules joined together. Polysaccharides are made from long chains of monosaccharides and include **starch, dextrin, cellulose** and **pectin**.

Sugar and sweeteners

White sugar	White sugar is a refined product that comes from sugar cane or sugar beet. This highly processed product is made using energy- and chemical-intensive processes. Refined white sugar provides empty calories with no nutrition. Monsanto's GM sugar beets make up 95% of the US crop, but GM beet is not approved for cultivation in the EU.
Demerara	Demerara is a light brown, partially refined sugar produced from the first crystallization during the processing of cane juice into sugar crystals. This is unlike brown sugar, which is refined white sugar with a bit of molasses added back into it.
Rapadura sugar	Of all the cane sugars, rapadura is the least processed. It is common in Brazil, Venezuela and the Caribbean. After extracting the pure juice from the sugar cane, it is evaporated over low heats and then finally ground to produce a grainy sugar. It is not cooked at high temperatures or spun to change it into crystals, and molasses is not separated out from the sugar.
Molasses	The syrup that is left after the process of precipitating out sugar crystals from sugar cane or sugar beets is known as molasses. To extract as much sugar as possible, the syrup is boiled three times, and with each successive cycle, the leftover molasses becomes darker and contains less sugar.
High-fructose corn syrup	The process that converts cornflour into a sweetener was discovered in the 1970s, and it has provided a cheap alternative to sugar in the food processing industry. Known as high-fructose corn syrup, or HFC, it has replaced sugar as a sweetener in carbonated drinks in the US and is a sweetener in a wide range of foods. HFC is made using an energy-intensive process of chemical fermentation and distillation. High consumption of high-fructose corn syrup correlates with a dramatic increase in a range of degenerative diseases including diabetes, heart disease and obesity.
Agave	Often thought of as a natural and healthy alternative to beet and cane sugar, agave is, generally, a highly-processed product: it is made by crushing the plant and converting the inulin to sugar either by heat or with enzymes. This converted liquid is then sent to a vacuum evaporation chamber to further concentrate the sugars. This process robs the agave syrup of many of the plant's original nutrients. Agave syrup is high in isolated fructose; in fact, up to 75% of the sugar content can be fructose, an excess of which can cause health problems.
Yacon syrup	Native to the South American Andes, yacon syrup is glucose-free. It is a sweetener that does not increase blood sugar levels, and because of this it is often used by diabetics or those with pre-diabetic conditions. Yacon syrup, like agave, is an inulin-derived sweetener and contains large amounts of fructose.

Coconut palm sugar	Palm sugars have a long history as sweeteners. Coconut palm sugar comes from the nectar collected from the coconut tree, which is boiled to produce sweet crystals. It is a sustainable sugar that requires little water and supports agroforestry; however, it is worth considering that if you have palm sugar you cannot have coconuts as well, as the flower bud which will become a coconut is destroyed. Other palms also produce sugars, generally from tapping the tree itself.
Barley malt syrup	Malted grains are mixed with water to allow the enzymes to break down the starch and protein – the insoluble fibre is removed and the sugary liquid is boiled to concentrate into a syrup. Barley malt sugar contains mostly maltose and is high on the glycaemic index. Brown rice syrup is another form of malt syrup, sometimes made with the addition of barley malt and also high on the glycaemic index.
Maple syrup	Maple trees are tapped and sap is collected and boiled. The syrup has a high concentration of minerals and many antioxidants. Maple syrup consists primarily of sucrose. Maple syrup is graded by colour; the darker colour is made from the last stages of the sap tapped from the maple tree.
Honey	Honey is food from bees. A colony must visit over two million flowers, flying over 55,000 miles, to make one pound of honey. For the sake of the bee (and the planet) we should only eat honey when there is enough to share in the hive. Honey is an absolute treasure.
Stevia	Originally from the highland region of Northern Paraguay and Southern Brazil, stevia is now grown around the world. Cargill has been instrumental in the development of the stevia market through its Truvia brand. There are a number of chemical processes used to create the refined white powder stevia, and genetically modified forms of stevia are being grown. Refined white powdered stevia has none of the health benefits of green leaf stevia powder. The healthiest and safest process uses only cold water for extraction. Alternatively, you can buy leaves that are carefully picked and dried and sold as pure stevia leaf. A little stevia goes a long way because it is very sweet.
Xylitol, erythritol, mannitol, sorbitol and glycerol	Sugar alcohols occur naturally in plants. Whilst some of these are extracted, like mannitol from seaweed, most are manufactured in a highly intensive industrial process from sugars and starches. They are used in commercially prepared processed foods, especially in reduced calorie and low-carbohydrate diet foods. This is because sugar alcohols are not fully absorbed into the body.
Saccharin, aspartame and sucralose	Made by a highly industrial process, these chemical sweeteners are completely artificial. They have been linked to a myriad of problems including cancer, digestive disorders, lack of vitality and general fogginess.

Blood-sugar imbalance

When you eat a meal, your blood sugar rises, which prompts your pancreas to release insulin into your bloodstream. Insulin sends a signal to your muscle cells, telling them to take up the excess sugar. Your muscle cells either use up the glucose as an energy source or store it in a slightly altered form called glycogen. When you haven't eaten for several hours, your blood sugar begins to fall; to restore balance your pancreas pumps out the hormone glucagon that converts the glycogen back into glucose and sends it back into your bloodstream. If all is working harmoniously, the pancreas produces just enough of these hormones at just the right time to keep blood glucose within optimal levels.

A diet high in sugar and refined carbohydrates, however, can cause a system malfunction, lead to insulin resistance and increase your risk of diabetes. When you eat these foods, it causes a spike in your blood sugar level, forcing your pancreas to counter-attack with a surge of insulin. If you persist in eating this type of diet, your pancreas has to pump out more and more insulin. Over time the ceaseless demand for the hormone can exhaust the gland, culminating in an inability to produce sufficient insulin. This extreme form of sugar imbalance is type 2 diabetes.

Without insulin, your body can't use glucose for fuel, so your body breaks down fats to use for energy. When your body breaks down fats, waste products called ketones are produced. Your body cannot tolerate a large amount of ketones, but finds it difficult to get rid of them, leading to a life-threatening condition known as ketoacidosis.

Figures from the International Diabetes Federation show that 387 million people worldwide are living with diabetes and many millions more are predisposing themselves to this disease. Until just a couple of centuries ago, apart from the seasonal abundance of fruit, most people only had minimal sweetness in their diet. Today, a diet of refined and heavily processed foods, especially white flour and sugar, far exceeds our body's metabolic ability to cope. It's not that the sweet taste isn't important, but it needs to come from whole foods and be in balance with all the other tastes, not dominate. Through diet and lifestyle, diabetes is preventable and research has shown it is even reversible.

The problem with fructose

Glucose and fructose sugars are metabolised differently. Glucose enters the bloodstream via the small intestine and the body releases insulin to help regulate it. On the other hand, fructose is processed in the liver. If too much fructose enters the liver, it is unable to process it all fast enough for the body to use as sugar. Instead, it converts the fructose into fats, releasing them into the bloodstream as triglycerides, which are a risk factor for heart disease.

Fructose also leads to leptin resistance. Leptin is a hormone produced to tell us when we are full. When we eat too much fructose, leptin is sometimes switched off and the normal appetite signalling system is circumvented. This is at least part of the reason why excess fructose consumption is associated with weight gain. Fructose also increases uric acid levels, which can lead to gout, and some people can develop kidney stones or kidney failure.

Naturally-occurring fructose in fruit and vegetables comes with fibre, enzymes, minerals, vitamins and antioxidants and does not generally cause the same problem as the added sugars and sweeteners that contain fructose and that are now so common in our diet.

dancing hormones

It is the unceasing dance of our hormones that is essential to keep our bodies balanced. Although present in only tiny amounts, hormones act on every cell in the body. Hormones can work alone, but they are also responsive to each other; their ability to maintain a rhythm and perform their delicate dance is greatly affected by an individual's lifestyle.

Hormones are very sensitive and affected by a whole range of circumstances brought about by modern living. Physical and emotional stress, toxins in the environment and in our food, hormone-disrupting chemicals and nutritional deficiencies will all affect the flow of the dance.

The reproductive, cardiovascular, respiratory, neurological, digestive, musculoskeletal and immune systems are all dependent on a balanced hormonal system. Hormones also govern our moods and our ability to think clearly. Imbalances can happen at any time, but they seem to be most common in early and later stages of life.

Hormones are secreted into the bloodstream by glands that are located throughout various parts of the body and then enter cells via receptor sites. The glands and hormones are most commonly referred to as the endocrine system.

If your hormones are in balance, you will most likely sleep well, have lots of energy, a healthy sex drive, strong immunity and a well-functioning digestive system. An imbalance can lead to an array of disorders including diabetes, adrenal fatigue and pre-menstrual tension.

Stress impacts very negatively on hormones. There are different forms of stress – emotional, dietary, pain, inflammatory – and they arise from a myriad of factors including too much work, financial worries, relationship problems, too much processed and junk food and exposure to chemicals and toxins in the environment.

Female hormonal imbalances are often related to stress response. The more stress you are under, the more it unbalances your cortisol levels, and when cortisol is triggered in excess it competes with progesterone, which means that progesterone is no longer able to balance oestrogen.

Men often dismiss the signs of hormonal imbalances as just a natural part of ageing. Subtle changes in the endocrine system in men as they age can cause a variety of conditions including bone mineral loss, decreased libido and/or sexual function, weight gain and depression. However, men at any age, through lifestyle, can suffer from hormonal-related health issues; for example adrenal exhaustion, which is a leading factor of insulin resistance and low testosterone levels.

Help keep your hormones in balance

- Eat plenty of vegetables, as their array of nutrients supports the glands of the endocrine system.
- Eat a diet rich in omega 3, 6 and 9 fatty acids: they greatly enhance the health of the endocrine system, helping to move hormones around the body.
- Eat organic food to eliminate unwanted chemicals and maximise nutrition.
- Support your liver, which needs to be in good working order to metabolise oestrogen – artichoke, beetroot, chlorophyll-rich leaves, garlic and dandelion are all good liver foods.
- Watch your weight! Oestrogen is produced by fat cells, so it will increase in proportion to body fat. Oestrogen dominance affects both men and women.
- Limit or, better still, cut out sugar, which plays havoc with the endocrine system.
- Spend time outside every day and spend time in nature as much as possible.
- Avoid environmental chemicals.
- Minimise alcohol intake.

<u>The endocrine system:</u>
Pituitary gland
Known as the 'master gland', the pituitary gland has two parts: the anterior pituitary and the posterior pituitary, releasing different hormones.

Anterior pituitary

Growth hormone – promotes growth in children and helps maintain healthy muscle and bone mass in adults.

Prolactin – stimulates milk production in women.

Adrenocorticotropic hormone – helps to reduce stress through production of cortisol.

Thyroid-stimulating hormone – helps to regulate the thyroid, thus maintaining a healthy metabolism.

Luteinizing hormone – regulates oestrogen in women and testosterone in men.

Follicle-stimulating hormone – stimulates the release of a woman's eggs and helps with sperm production in men.

Posterior pituitary

Oxytocin – promotes contractions in pregnant women at the appropriate time and milk flow.

Antidiuretic hormone – regulates water balance in the body.

Hypothalamus – releases hormones that control the pituitary hormones.

Thymus gland – secretes hormones to make sure a person develops a healthy immune system.

Pineal gland – produces melatonin, which is the hormone that helps you sleep.

Testes – in men produce testosterone, which develops male sexual organs and traits.

Ovaries – in women produce the hormones oestrogen and progesterone.

Thyroid – hormones regulate metabolism and energy production.

Adrenal glands – two glands that sit on top of your kidneys and are made up of two distinct parts. The outer part of the gland, the adrenal cortex, secretes aldosterone, which regulates water retention in the body, and cortisone, which raises the level of sugar in the blood. The adrenal medulla, the inner part of the gland, produces adrenaline and noradrenaline, the fight or flight hormones.

Parathyroid – helps control calcium and phosphorous levels in the body.

Pancreas – releases insulin, which maintains healthy blood sugar levels.

nourishing families

Young ones

Diverse foods, naturally farmed and minimally processed, are the ones most likely to have all the right nutrients to support a child's development. Food, of course, sustained us long before we knew about nutrients, which were first discovered early in the 19th century by William Proust, who identified the 'macronutrients' protein, fat and carbohydrate. Early in the 20th century, Polish biochemist Casimir Funck isolated and named vitamins, and since then we have gone on to discover a staggering number of compounds in food.

The discovery and subsequent understanding of the different roles of individual nutrients in food have undoubtedly saved millions of lives. Paradoxically, however, with these discoveries food began to shift from being a natural product of the land to a product of food science, with many of the resulting processed foods being responsible for the huge rise in degenerative diseases. Societies that eat food from the land are largely free of these diseases, and this is regardless of whether it is a high animal protein diet like that of the Canadian Eskimos or a wild plant-based diet like the !Kung of the Kalahari desert, the common factor being that the food is natural and only processed in time-honoured ways to preserve and maximise nutrition.

Young children need plenty of energy from regular meals and healthy snacks, and, as they are unable to eat large quantities, food should be as nutrient-dense as possible. Good-quality protein, unrefined carbohydrates, the right fats and plenty of colourful vegetables and fruits will ensure the right nutrients are in the food your young ones eat. Ensuring meals include the important fats that support the growing brain and avoiding sugar are two key considerations.

Brain fats

The right fats are crucially important, and both the lack of and the wrong balance can have long-lasting implications for a child. Healthy brains are about 60% structural fat, and as the brain grows, it selects the necessary building blocks from among the fatty acids that are available in the food a child eats. Research has shown that children's brains are built differently depending on the foods that they are fed when they are rapidly growing.

Numerous studies have shown the impact that the two **essential fatty acids (EFAs)**, **linoleic acid (LA)** and **alpha-linolenic acid (ALA)**, have on the brain and how important they are for mental development and balanced behaviour.

The most prevalent structural fats in the brain are **arachidonic acid (AA)**, synthesised from linoleic acid, and **docosahexaenoic acid (DHA)**, synthesised from alpha-linolenic acid. DHA is particularly critical for vision, making up over 30% of the retina. Photo-receptor cells require DHA to convert light into an electric signal. Deficiencies of DHA interfere with the functioning of the chemical messengers – neurotransmitters – and also impair both cardiovascular and immune system functioning. AA is found in eggs, fish and meat, or it is synthesised from LA. DHA is found in algae and fish or synthesised from LNA. Some of the best foods for obtaining the EFAs LA and LNA are hemp, flax, pumpkin and walnut.

Sugar

In terms of evolution, our sweet tooth can be explained by the association of the sweet taste with high-energy foods, which would in the past have been important for our survival. However, this evolution happened long ago when food was scarce. Today, with a great variety of foods full of sugar readily available in Western countries, the preference for these foods brings many disadvantages.

So as not to encourage the sweet tooth tendency, young children should avoid sugar; ripe seasonal fruit is all the sweet taste they need. It is best not to give young children fruit juices; it is far better to eat the whole fruit as this allows the fibre to slow down the absorption of the fruit sugar fructose. As they grow older and spend time away from home, it may become harder to avoid sweet puddings, cakes and biscuits, but at least in the home you can make sure you only offer these foods occasionally. Poor eating habits at home set children up for long-term physical and behavioural problems.

Adolescents

Young people have a spurt of growth at puberty – for girls this is between 11–15 years and for boys, 13–16 years. Good nutrition is very important, and there are two nutrients – iron and calcium – that are often at risk of deficiency.

Iron

Iron deficiency among adolescents, especially girls, is quite common. It is estimated that almost 25% of 15–18-year-old girls have an iron deficiency. Iron is vital for the function of red blood cells and for the synthesis of adenosine triphosphate, or ATP, the body's primary source of cellular energy, absolutely essential in supporting adolescent development. Among girls, menstruation increases the risk for iron deficiency. Untreated iron deficiency can lead to iron deficiency anaemia, resulting in severe fatigue.

Dietary iron exists in two forms – haem and non-haem iron. Haem iron is found in animal foods and is generally well absorbed. Non-haem iron, from plant foods, is less reliable, as other food components, such as tannins in tea and phytates in some cereals, can hinder its absorption. Vitamin C (found in a variety of fruits and vegetables) as well as malic acid (found in plums and apples) and citric acid (found in citrus fruits) enhance the absorption of non-haem iron.

Adolescents need to eat plenty of iron-rich foods such as whole grains, nuts, seeds, dried fruits and green leafy vegetables (and if they choose, lean meats and fish). The best sources of plant-based iron include cocoa, dried apricots and oatmeal.

Calcium

99% of all calcium in the body is in our bones, and they grow rapidly during adolescence. In fact, about 45% of the adult skeletal mass is formed during this period, and all the calcium from this growth must come from the food being eaten.

Ensuring the right intake of calcium from a balanced diet will reduce the risk of osteoporosis in later years. Particularly good sources of calcium include kale, white beans, broccoli, almonds, cabbage, watercress, yoghurt, kefir and small fish, if you eat the bones.

No nutrient works in isolation; other vitamins and minerals, like Vitamin D and phosphorous, are also needed for building bones. Physical activity also helps to build bone mass and density. Many activities during adolescence – including cycling, skating, gymnastics, ball games and dancing – will help build strong bones.

Family meals

Around the family table, children learn the stories behind the meals they share and grow a deep appreciation for the food they eat. By sharing local, wholesome food, children are nourished and sustained by relationships that bring comfort, conviviality and community into their young lives, helping them to grow into loving, thoughtful, creative and energetic beings.

Families are no longer solely made up of married parents living with their children; today they are an eclectic mix, including second marriage families through to single child with one parent families. Each family constellation presents its own individual challenges, from meeting the preferences of a number of diverse children through to juggling the needs of work and home.

Eating together is vitally important. Encouraging research undertaken by Sheffield University found that the family meal remains a widely shared aspiration and that the implication of a wholesale decline in family eating is based on questionable evidence.

There are invariably obstacles to sharing food in the evenings; adults may arrive home late, young children are tired and hungry, older children are most likely on their way out. Compromises may have to be made, but with a little forward planning, it is often possible to create a rhythm that makes our aspirations of eating together more the norm than the exception.

If weekdays are just a bit too hectic, create a particularly special coming together at the weekends. Take time to really enjoy cooking and sharing breakfasts on Saturday and Sunday. Children can join in with the preparations every step of the way; if you have teenagers, you might find this idea works better as a brunch!

family breakfasts

SPRING

Buckwheat pancakes ⓔ

Serves 4

A firm favourite with children. There are so many different filling options. Make two or three different ones so everyone has one they really like.

This is also a brilliant recipe for involving children in the kitchen; they will soon become very adept at pancake making. All that flipping and filling is hungry work, so make plenty.

110g buckwheat flour
25g cornflour
2 eggs
275ml gluten free oat milk
little olive oil

Place the flours into a bowl. Add the eggs and milk, beat until smooth, and season. Set aside to rest for 10 minutes. Heat a smidgeon of oil in a small frying pan. Add a little of the batter mixture and tip to coat the base of the pan. Cook for 2–3 minutes until golden. Flip over and cook the other side for a further 1–2 minutes. Slide onto a plate and keep warm. Repeat with the remaining batter to make 8 pancakes in total. Take to the table and start filling!

<u>Filling suggestions:</u>
wilted spinach and feta
mashed fava beans with mint
purple sprouting broccoli with garlic
yoghurt and honey
egg mayonnaise with black olives
sprouted alfalfa, green leaves and tahini

Summer berries with almond cream and breakfast scones ⓝ ⓓ ⓔ ⓖ

Serves 4

If you do not have your own fruit in the garden, visit a 'pick your own' farm and while away a few hours with the children, stocking up on vivid, ripe berries and coming away with a red-stained mouth and hands. This is a lovely breakfast for a summer morning: bright summer jewels in a sparkling glass with a wedge of scone warm from the oven.

To serve
700g berries

For the almond cream
200g almonds, blanched, skinned and soaked
    in cold water for 12 hours
180ml water
½ teaspoon vanilla

For the breakfast scone
350g spelt flour
2 teaspoons baking powder
110g butter
2 tablespoons rapadura sugar
zest of 1 lemon
110g seeds – e.g. sunflower and pumpkin
225g yoghurt
1 egg, beaten

<u>To make the almond cream:</u>
Blend all the ingredients together in a high-speed processor. Place in a bowl and chill.

<u>To make the scone:</u>
Set the oven to 200°C/400°F/Gas mark 6.
    Mix the flour and baking powder together. Cut the butter into small pieces and rub into the flour until it resembles fine breadcrumbs. Add the sugar, lemon and seeds and stir well. Add the yoghurt to the dry ingredients, stirring until it gathers into a ball. Turn the dough out onto a floured board and shape into a round,

about 20cm across. Place on a lightly buttered baking sheet and cut the round into 8 wedges. Brush well with beaten egg and bake for 25 minutes.

<u>To serve:</u>
Arrange the fruit in 4 glass bowls.
Serve with the breakfast scone and almond cream.

....

AUTUMN

Mushrooms, wilted greens, poached egg and rye toast Ⓔ Ⓖ Ⓢ

Serves 4

Early morning mist, the scent of autumn and shrieks of delight as children discover field mushrooms breaking through in the meadow. If you are lucky enough to live where field mushrooms grow, it's well worth picking them for breakfast. If you don't, buy a mix of oyster, shiitake and chestnut mushrooms. If your children are going through a 'won't eat greens' phase, cook the greens separately so they can just have mushrooms. Unless of course it's a 'won't eat mushrooms' phase too, in which case it's just a delicious poached egg on rye toast!

225g fresh mushrooms
olive oil
4 handfuls of greens (e.g. spinach, watercress,
    dandelion, oriental mustard, young cavolo
    nero) picked over and large stalks removed
1 dessert spoon tamari
4 eggs
4 slices of rye toast
salt and pepper

Cut the mushrooms into thick slices and cook in a little olive oil over a medium heat for 4 minutes. Add the greens and allow them to wilt. Add the tamari and season well.

Bring a wide, shallow pan of water to a gentle simmer and add a pinch of salt. Crack an egg into a cup and gently pour in one movement into the water. Repeat with the rest of the eggs. Cook for 2–3 minutes. Whilst the eggs are cooking, pile the mushrooms and greens onto the toast, then lift the eggs out and put on top.

WINTER

Cassoulet ⓢ

Serves 6–8

This is a winner for a long, convivial, extended family Sunday breakfast. The beans will sit happily in the fridge for a couple of days, and then all that needs to happen is for you to arrange the potato slices on top (or, if you prefer, you can use the classic cassoulet breadcrumbs) and stick it in the oven. For an even more sumptuous dish, you could top each serving with a poached egg. Serve with a big green and sprouted seed salad.

400g dried haricot or cannellini beans
2 red onions, finely chopped
4 celery sticks, chopped
4 cloves garlic, chopped
4 carrots, chopped
4 tablespoons olive oil
400g tin chopped tomatoes
1 piece of wakame seaweed
2 bay leaves
1 tablespoon thyme, chopped
6 sage leaves, finely chopped
500g winter squash, peeled, seeded and cut
    into chunks
1 teaspoon cumin
1 tablespoon mustard seed
1 tablespoon tamari
1 large baking potato
extra olive oil
salt and pepper

Soak the beans overnight, drain, cover with cold water and bring to a boil. Simmer for 10 minutes, cover tightly and set aside.

Gently cook the onions, celery, garlic and carrots in 3 tablespoons of the olive oil until soft, then add the tomatoes, wakame and herbs.

Drain the beans, reserving the liquid, and stir into the tomato mixture, adding enough of the reserved liquid to make sure the beans are completely immersed in the liquid. Simmer gently for an hour.

Toss the squash in a tablespoon of olive oil, season with cumin, salt and black pepper and roast until tender and crisp.

When the beans are cooked, stir in the mustard seed, tamari and squash, adding liquid as necessary to make the beans really moist. Turn into a baking dish, cool and refrigerate.

Next day, finely slice the potato, season and rub with olive oil. Arrange overlapping on top of the beans and bake in a moderately hot oven for 45 minutes until golden brown.

grow, cook, share

Children love to grow, cook and proudly share the food they have prepared. These sensual experiences create a framework for children to become part of a food culture that creates well-being for both themselves and the planet.

Grow

Growing vegetables together gives children a chance to discover and experience nature's basic patterns and rhythms. From soil to seed to plant to food to compost and back to soil – an inspiring journey in which children readily engage. There are many different ways children can join in, either in your own garden, a community garden or growing on the windowsill. Cut-and-come-again salads are easy and relatively quick to grow, and they encourage children to eat green leaves; young ones seem to especially like pea shoots. Growing tomatoes that can be turned into tomato sauce for a freshly baked pizza is always popular. From an early age, children really enjoy being involved in composting, and if you don't have a garden or access to communal composting, put a wormery, which children find endlessly fascinating, on the back doorstep!

Cook

Children love to be involved in the alchemy of the kitchen. Helping to prepare food greatly influences their preferences for nutritious and delicious food. From early beginnings sitting in a high chair playing with different colours and textures, a familiarity with ingredients grows. Before long, children will be mixing, stirring, peeling, grating, cutting and chopping their way to becoming confident young cooks. Of course, it will take longer to prepare a meal with little ones helping, and it generally makes rather a mess... but does this really matter when the benefits are so enormous? Eating habits and taste preferences are formed from a very early age, so a variety of foods is very important from the outset. Being part of the process of choosing and preparing food will grow an understanding and love of real food.

Share

Sharing food together around the table gives children the opportunity from an early age to respect the soil that nourishes us, have gratitude for the food they eat and maintain a deep appreciation of all those who have had a hand in bringing the food to the table. Sharing food, with all its traditions, customs and social implications, is an intrinsic part of human development. Children derive huge pleasure from the knowledge that they have been involved in the preparation of the food that is being shared. There are times when circumstances can prevent gathering together around the table every day, but there are always other times when you will be able to share a meal with one another. Joyful conversations and stories are an important part of the mutual nurturing we experience when we give ourselves the time and space to share food together.

seven flavours of summer

Rose

There are so many different roses, but the heady, sensual smell of the Gallica rose so evokes the summer. The petals add a heavenly fragrance to summer dishes, and flavoured vinegars and syrups bring a little summer sunshine into the dark winter. The Latin word *rosa* comes from the Greek word for rose – *rhódon*. It was probably the flower's deep colour that suggested the fable of the rose springing from the blood of Adonis.

Raspberry

According to legend, raspberries were originally white. The nymph Ida pricked her finger while picking berries for the crying infant Jupiter, and raspberries were stained red with her blood. Actually, white varieties can still be found, as well as yellow ones.

Raspberries are nutritional powerhouses. They are packed with soluble fibre – a good source of folic acid, beta-carotene and Vitamin C. It's hard to improve on the near perfection of eating a bowl of fresh raspberries in the summer sun.

Elderflower

For thousands of years, all parts of this tree have been used medicinally. The benefits are so varied and valuable that the elder has been called the 'medicine chest' tree. Gathering armfuls of fragrant flowers is part of the magic of summer. Pick the creamy blossom heads on a sunny day. Dry some by spreading them thinly in an airy room until dry and crumbly. Rub and shake them to separate the flowers from the stalks, then store the petals in an airtight dark jar and use to make infusions. Turn the rest into delicious drinks and puddings.

Basil

There are more than 60 varieties of basil, all of which differ somewhat in appearance and taste. Generally fragrant, warming and deliciously pungent, it is one of the summer season's most versatile herbs. The bright flavour enlivens egg, vegetable and fruit dishes and makes a change to mint in a mojito. Basil is a stimulant and digestive, good for settling an upset stomach and relieving nausea.

Cucumber

Cucumbers are sweet-flavoured and cooling in the summer heat. Both the whole cucumber and the juice soothe inflammatory conditions including digestive inflammation, sore throat and inflamed skin conditions; the juice is particularly useful applied to burns, especially sunburn. Cucumber skin is rich in silicon and has a bitter edge. Silicon is a vital trace mineral required by the body for strong and flexible joints, glowing skin and strong bones.

Tomato

Sun-ripened tomatoes and the unforgettable smell of tomato foliage are the tastes and aromas of summer. The many health benefits of tomatoes can be attributed to their wealth of nutrients and vitamins, including an impressive amount of Vitamins A, C and K, as well as significant amounts of Vitamin B6, folate, and thiamine. Organic tomatoes have an amazing array of phytonutrients because they have not been doused in chemicals.

Nasturtium

A showy summer flower that adds a vibrant flourish to dishes, nasturtium has been used in the kitchen for centuries. Nasturtium leaves, buds and flowers add a sharp, peppery bite to salads. The pickled seeds are often described as tasting like roasted capers. The leaves contain significant levels of Vitamin C and iron. Medicinally, they are used to break up congestion in the respiratory system. The leaves have a tonic, cleansing and antiseptic effect. They are so easy to grow; buy a packet of seeds and grow them in the garden or in a pot.

the industrialisation of soya and corn

Diane Osgood

Most of us eat a lot of corn, soya, wheat and rice. In fact, according to Michael Pollan, Americans consume 811 calories – or 40% of their average daily caloric intake – from foods derived from corn and soya alone. Much of the corn and soya is integrated into processed foods as fillers, starch, stabilisers, sweeteners and oils, so we don't recognise them on our plate. As a result, we may not be aware of how much corn and soya is actually in our diet. If we consider, in addition, the content of the feed for animals that become our meat, our indirect consumption of these two crops is tremendously high.

Human health concerns aside, the increasing reliance on a handful of crops for much of our food has serious implications. Our agricultural systems currently focus on a limited selection of crops and a narrowing genetic diversity within that small group of key crops. This means that farmers plant the same variety of one crop over millions of acres. This lack of diversity makes it hard for production to bounce back if a major pest, such as a virus, bacteria or insect, successfully invades production zones – something now happening with bananas. Although bananas come in thousands of varieties, one single variety, the Cavendish, dominates 45% of global crop production and 95% of all bananas exported to western markets. Recently, a fungus strain hit the Cavendish banana crop in Asia, the Middle East and Africa and is killing them all, putting the income of millions of farmers at risk.

As agriculture devotes more land to soya and corn production, we lose acreage for other important crops, including wheat, oats, sorghum and barley. The US converted roughly 1.3 million acres of grasslands to corn/soya monocultures in 2006–2011. The loss of waterways, wetlands and the plant and animal species that reside there are just a few of the consequences of this conversion.

The number of commercial seed sources is shrinking globally. The 'big four' biotech seed companies – Monsanto, DuPont Pioneer, Syngenta and Dow AgroSciences – own over 80% of the US corn and soya market and an estimated 60% of the European corn market. The concentration of ownership of genetically engineered (GE) seeds is stark. Almost 80% of US corn is GE, and of this, 95% contains Monsanto's traits. We are witnessing the results when shareholders and executives, rather than farmers and consumers, decide what goes onto our plates.

How did this happen?

The remarkable rise of soya and corn production is the story of agriculture's industrialisation. Today, farmers grow soya for its component parts – oil, extruded protein and fibre – which go into processed food, feedlot animal fodder and manufactured materials, such as paints and plastics. It wasn't always this way. Soya was introduced in the US and Europe as animal fodder and green manure. During WWII, soya became a critical source of oil for civilian food and wartime industry, causing production to more than quadruple in a few years. After the war, persistent scientific and engineering efforts led to more palatable uses of the oil, including margarine. It is now by far the most important edible fat and animal fodder in the west.

The rise of corn is likewise linked to industrial production. It mainly goes into animal feedlots, high-fructose corn syrup, ethanol and bio-plastics. Synthetic fertilisers, irrigation, cheap land and large farm equipment systems make it possible for farmers to manage hundreds of thousands of acres; government subsidies and tax breaks often provide further support.

US agriculture has widely adopted genetically engineered soya and corn. Industrial agriculture won the right to keep GE crops mixed with non-GE crops, a major victory that put the onus on organic and non-GE farmers to keep their crops from being segregated. In many ways, this one decision propelled GE crops so deeply into our food system that it will now take significant action to unlock our food systems from them.

What can we do?

Remember, we are the economy. Each purchase we make sends a signal that, when joined by others, creates the demand to which the market responds. Carlos Petrini, the founder and president of Slow Food International, challenges us to be co-creators of our food systems, not just passive consumers. I agree. Those of us who value fresh, healthy, chemical-free food need to join together with farmers, food producers, retailers and our political representatives to co-create the food systems we want. We need to take positive action.

- Support farmers and crop diversity in your area by shopping at farmers' markets.
- Ask questions: Where does this food come from? What is in it?
- Write to your grocery stores and ask for more foods without processed ingredients.
- Grow your own heirloom vegetables and fruits to support diversity.
- Learn about agricultural and food subsidies and engage your elected representatives to understand their impacts and alternatives.

Industrial food reflects the era in which it developed, a time when rapid industrial growth, advancements in chemistry and life sciences, the need for oils and cheap fats drove the market. That era has passed. Today, we understand the critical importance of living sustainably and our intimate interdependence with the web of life on our beautiful planet. It's up to us to ensure that today's food systems reflect our era.

Diane Osgood is an environmental economist who has been at the forefront of corporate engagement on the environment and human rights for over twenty years.

summer recipes

Red pepper, basil, celery and cucumber juice
Red grape and spirulina juice
Summer smoothie
Rose syrup
Redcurrant syrup
Strawberry breakfast Ⓝ
Pea soup Ⓓ
Rainbow salad
Summer vegetable and pickled ginger sushi
rolls with red chilli dipping sauce Ⓢ
Courgette noodles with harissa, tomatoes
and flat-leaf parsley
Fennel with nasturtiums
Pickled marsh samphire
Tomato and garlic flatbreads Ⓖ
Blueberry tart Ⓝ
Date paste
Rum pot
Almond milk with rose and cardamom Ⓝ
Lime flower tea

Ⓖ *– contains gluten*
Ⓓ *– contains dairy*
Ⓢ *– contains soya*
Ⓔ *– contains eggs*
Ⓝ *– contains nuts*

Red pepper, basil, celery and cucumber juice

Serves 1
½ cucumber
2 celery sticks with leaves
handful of basil
½ deseeded red pepper

Do not peel the cucumber, as many valuable compounds are in the skin. Juice the celery leaves as well, as they contain many nutritional benefits. Prepare to be mentally stimulated by the basil!

Cut the pepper, celery and cucumber to fit the machine feeder. Put all the ingredients through the machine. Pour into a glass and drink at once.

Red grape and spirulina juice

Serves 1
1 heaped teaspoon spirulina
250g red grapes

Place the spirulina in a glass. Juice the grapes. Mix the spirulina to a paste with a little of the juice before slowly adding the remaining juice, stirring well. Drink straight away.

Summer smoothie

Serves 1
handful of strawberries, hulled
handful of raspberries
1 peach, stone removed and cut into quarters
1 tablespoon rose syrup
rose petals and borage flowers

Put all the ingredients into a blender and blend until smooth. Pour into a glass over crushed ice. Top with a few rose petals and a couple of borage flowers.

Rose syrup

225g Gallica rose petals
juice of 1 lemon
300g sugar
525ml water

Put the rose petals in a large bowl and pour over the lemon juice. With your fingers, gently massage to slightly soften. Add the sugar, mix well and leave overnight.

In the morning, boil the water and pour over the mixture, then leave for a further 12 hours.

Strain through a fine sieve or muslin, then gently bring to the boil. Remove from heat and pour into warm sterilised bottles. Seal with screw caps or corks.

....

Redcurrant syrup

1.25kg redcurrants, removed from stems
275ml water
peel of 1 lemon
peel of 1 orange
demerara sugar to taste

Simmer the redcurrants in the water with the orange and lemon peel until soft. Strain and measure the liquid and add 350g sugar to each 550ml. Return to pan. Bring to the boil and simmer for 30 minutes. Bottle or freeze. Lovely with lemon geranium cake (see page 89), vanilla ice cream, or as a warm fireside drink in the middle of the winter.

Strawberry breakfast Ⓝ

Serves 1
handful of sprouted buckwheat
1 tablespoon hemp seeds
1 tablespoon pumpkin seeds
1 tablespoon sunflower seeds
1 dessert spoon honey
110g almond milk
12 strawberries
1 tablespoon ground flax

Soak the buckwheat and seeds with the honey in the almond milk overnight. To serve, add the strawberries and top with ground flax.

....

Pea soup Ⓓ

Serves 4–6
6 spring onions, sliced
50g butter
1.35kg fresh peas, shelled
1.2 litres vegetable stock
6 mint leaves
salt and pepper
handful of mint

Soften the spring onions in the butter. Tip in the peas, stock and mint and bring to the boil; simmer gently for about 10 minutes. Purée until smooth in a blender or with a stick blender, then return to the pan. Check the seasoning and heat through.

Pour into bowls and top with the mint.

Rainbow Salad

Serves 2
The following is merely a suggestion of how you can make a salad with all the colours of the rainbow. Create your own version with the vegetables of your choice. The salad is big enough for two, so share the joy with a friend.

For the salad
1 tomato
1 carrot
1 green courgette
1 yellow pepper
1 fennel bulb
¼ red cabbage

For the dressing
8 tablespoons olive oil
4 tablespoons cider vinegar
2 teaspoons honey
¼ teaspoon salt
1 teaspoon whole grain mustard
freshly ground black pepper

To serve
large handful of sunflower sprouts
borage flowers
mint sprigs

Cut all the vegetables into bite-sized pieces and put into a large bowl. Whisk the dressing ingredients together and gently toss the vegetables with enough dressing to generously coat. Mix in the sunflower sprouts, divide between 2 bowls and top with borage flowers and mint.

Summer vegetable and pickled ginger sushi rolls with red chilli dipping sauce ⓢ

Serves 6

6 sheets of toasted nori
12 tablespoons sticky brown rice, flavoured
    with 1 tablespoon each of mirin and
    brown rice vinegar
2 carrots, cut into fine matchsticks
1 yellow pepper, cut into fine matchsticks
2 small courgettes, cut into fine matchsticks
1 tablespoon tamari
sunflower seed sprouts
12 slices of pickled ginger, cut into thin slices

Place a sheet of nori onto a piece of greaseproof paper (or a bamboo sushi mat if you have one) with the shorter side facing you. Cover thinly with rice, spreading to the side edge but leaving 4cm at the top and around a centimeter at the bottom. Lay the matchstick vegetables on top of the rice, cover with sunflower seed sprouts, splash with a little tamari and top it all with the pickled ginger.

Carefully roll up the nori until a tight cylinder is formed, and leave wrapped up in greaseproof paper until ready to serve.

Gently unwrap the sushi and cut each roll into 5 pieces. Serve with the sweet chilli dipping sauce opposite.

Sweet chilli dipping sauce

50g honey
50ml water
1 tablespoon cider vinegar
1 red chilli (choose your variety depending on
    how hot you want your dipping sauce),
    finely chopped
half a thumb-sized piece of ginger, peeled
    and grated
2 cloves garlic, peeled and very finely chopped

Put the honey, water and vinegar into a small saucepan and gently
heat, stirring constantly. Bring to the boil and cook for a minute.
Add the chilli, garlic and ginger and cook for 2 minutes, stirring
occasionally. Remove from the heat and leave to cool.

....

Pickled ginger

2 large pieces of ginger, peeled and very
    finely sliced
1 tablespoon sea salt
110g cider vinegar
50g honey
2 small beetroots, juiced

Toss the ginger in a bowl with the salt. Bring the cider vinegar,
honey and beetroot juice to the boil, tip in the ginger and simmer
gently until syrupy. Put into a clean jar and secure with a lid. Keep in
the fridge.

Courgette noodles with harissa, tomatoes and flat-leaf parsley

Serves 6
6 courgettes
6 teaspoons harissa
55ml olive oil
450g cherry tomatoes
bunch flat-leaf parsley

You can either use a spiralizer to make the noodles (a reasonably inexpensive hand tool, which is great fun for children to use) or alternatively slice into thin ribbons and then fine long noodles with a sharp knife.

Pile the noodles into a bowl. Mix the harissa and olive oil together, then gently mix into the noodles with your hands, making sure they are all coated. Leave to marinate for half an hour.

Cut the tomatoes in half. Pick the leaves off the parsley. Just before serving, mix through the tomatoes and parsley and divide between plates.

....

Harissa

1 teaspoon caraway seeds
1 teaspoon cumin seeds
1 teaspoon coriander seeds
8 red chillies, seeded and chopped
2 roasted red peppers, seeded and skinned
4 cloves garlic
½ teaspoon salt
3 tablespoons olive oil
1 tablespoon lemon juice

Dry roast the caraway, cumin and coriander until the fragrance fills the air. Be attentive at all times, shaking the pan so the seeds do not burn. Put the spices, chillies, pepper, garlic, salt, olive oil and lemon juice in a processor and process to a smooth paste, adding more oil if too dry. Put into sterilised jars, leaving a centimetre at the top, and cover with olive oil. Keep refrigerated and use within 6 weeks.

Fennel with nasturtiums

Serves 6
4 small handfuls of nasturtium seed pods
brine (15g salt mixed with 250ml water)
150ml (approx.) apple cider vinegar
6 fennel bulbs
2 tablespoons olive oil
salt and pepper

For the dressing
3 tablespoons olive oil
1 teaspoon wholegrain mustard
1 teaspoon apple cider vinegar
black pepper
6 nasturtium flowers

Gather the fresh, green seed pods of the nasturtium from the flowers on a warm day. Make a brine by dissolving the salt in the water. Put the nasturtium seeds in a bowl, pour over the brine, and leave for 24 hours. Drain the seeds, pat dry and put in a glass bowl. Cover with cider vinegar and put aside.

Remove the green fronds from the fennel and reserve. Remove the 2 outer leaves of the fennel bulb and reserve for stock, soup or juicing. Bring a pan of water to the boil and drop in the fennel bulbs. Simmer for 5 minutes, then remove and cool. The water is a base for a very tasty stock.

Slice each fennel bulb lengthways into 3 equal parts. Place the fennel pieces on a baking tray and rub with olive oil, season with salt and black pepper, pop into the oven at 200°C/400°F/Gas mark 6 and cook until golden brown.

Transfer the fennel to a serving dish. Whisk the olive oil, mustard and vinegar together and pour over the salad. Scatter over 3 tablespoons of nasturtium seed pods. Tear over the fennel fronds, give a good twist of black pepper and finally, on top of the salad, place the vibrant nasturtium flowers.

Any extra nasturtium pods will keep covered with cider vinegar in the fridge for at least 6 weeks.

Pickled marsh samphire

4 big handfuls of marsh samphire
water to cover
cider vinegar
4 small chillies
2 bay leaves
1 teaspoon peppercorns

Wash the samphire really well and cut off any roots and hard stalks.
Put into a pan and cover with water, then add 2 tablespoons vinegar.
Bring to the boil and then simmer for 3 minutes. Drain and pack into
sterilised preserving jars. Add the spices and cover with vinegar, and
seal tightly with vinegar-proof lids. It's ready to use straight away,
but will keep and is always welcome as a relish in the winter months.

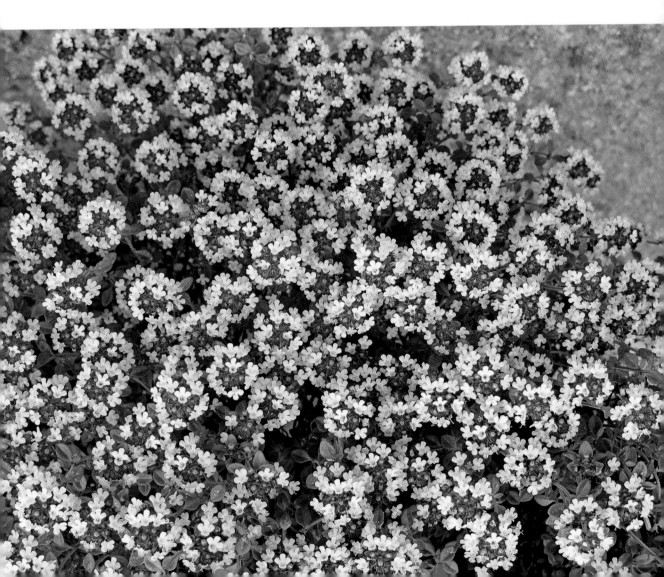

Tomato and garlic flatbreads Ⓖ

For the flatbread
15g yeast
100ml tepid water
1 teaspoon honey
250g wholemeal spelt
1 teaspoon fine sea salt
100ml olive oil
extra water

For the tomato and garlic topping
6 tomatoes, quartered, seeded and diced,
    mixed with 4 garlic cloves, chopped

Mix the yeast, water and honey together and set aside. In a bowl, combine the flour and salt. Add the yeast mixture, half the olive oil and enough water to make a soft, sticky dough. Cover and leave for 10 minutes. Put half the remaining olive oil in a large bowl, tip in the dough and knead gently for 5 minutes. Cover and leave for 1 hour.

Rub a little of the remaining oil on a work surface, then pat the dough to a rectangle and fold it in by thirds each way, flip over and cover. Leave for 30 minutes and repeat the process 2 more times.

Lightly oil a baking tray, approx. 13x18 cm. Gently roll or pat out the dough to fit the tray. Scatter over the tomato and garlic mixture, cover and leave for 20 minutes. Bake in the centre of a hot oven (220°C/425°F/Gas mark 7) for about 30 minutes or until golden brown.

Blueberry tart ⓝ

Serves 8
For the crust
110g coconut butter
3 tablespoons date paste (see below)
275g ground almonds
110g walnuts, very finely chopped
55g maple syrup

For the cream
225g cashews, soaked for 2 hours
1 tablespoon honey
2 tablespoons coconut butter
2 teaspoons vanilla extract

For the topping
450g blueberries

Lightly oil a plate and set a 23cm flan ring on top. Soften the coconut butter, then add the remaining crust ingredients and mix well. When thoroughly mixed, press evenly onto the plate and up the side of the flan ring to create an even thickness of crust. Put into the fridge for at least an hour to set.

Blend together all the ingredients for the cream in a high-speed blender.

Carefully remove the flan ring from the crust. Fill the tart with the cream almost to the top, level and chill for 2 hours. Pile the blueberries on top of the cream before serving.

....

Date paste

Soak a handful of dates for at least 2 hours in just enough water to cover. Remove the dates from the water and whizz in a processor, adding just enough water to make a soft paste. It will last, covered in the fridge, for a couple of weeks.

Rum pot

A scrumptious way to preserve the fruits of the season, and a good standby for a celebration. The rum pot originated in Germany, where traditionally a large stoneware jar called a *rumtopf* would be used. These aren't too difficult to find, but you can also use a Kilner jar. It's traditional to start with the first fruits of the growing season, so I generally start with gooseberries and strawberries, move on to apricots, cherries and raspberries, then black, red and white currants, blueberries and finally blackberries, plums, apples and pears. Gooseberries need topping and tailing, strawberries need hulling, fruits with stones need them removed and currants need to be stripped from their stems.

Start by putting a layer of your prepared fruit in the bottom of your pot. It is preferable not to wash the fruit. If you do, gently dry. For every 450g of fruit, stir in 50g rapadura sugar and cover the fruit plus an inch with good-quality rum. Every time a new fruit comes into season, repeat this process until your pot is full. Stand in a cool, dry place away from direct sunlight for 6–8 weeks.

This is brilliant for a Christmas or New Year celebration. Strain out the fruit, and you have the most delicious liquor on its own or as a cocktail base. The fruits can be used over ice cream and sorbets, with cakes, or just by themselves.

Almond milk with rose and cardamom ⓝ

Makes 1 generous glass or 2 smaller glasses
50g skinned almonds, soaked
225ml ice-cold water
¼ teaspoon ground cardamom
1 tablespoon rose syrup

Place the almonds and water in a blender and whizz together. If you prefer a really smooth drink, strain them and then put the milk back in the blender with the remaining ingredients and whizz it all together.

Lime flower tea

The lime tree flowers in late June or July. Gather the flowers, including the wing-like bracts at the base, while in full bloom and lay them out to dry in a warm, airy room for 3–4 weeks. Lime flower tea has a honey taste, and a soothing effect on the digestive and nervous system. Drink in the evening to encourage sleep.

Place 6 fresh lime flowers or a dessertspoon of dried lime flowers into a pot or jug, cover with half a litre of boiling water and leave to infuse for 10 minutes.

autumn

healthy immune system

Our immune system is truly remarkable. Within just a single minute it has the ability to produce a million specific antibodies and to recognise and disarm a billion different harmful invaders. Bone marrow, the lymphatic system, the thymus, liver and spleen all play a very important role in this, but the health of the immune system is cradled in the healthy bacterial flora (microbiota) that live in the gut.

A healthy gut wall is packed full of lymphocytes poised to jump into action and protect the body if the need arises. Lymphocytes produce immunoglobulins, and the most important immunoglobulin in the gut is Secretory Immunoglobulin A (IgA), which protects the body from unwelcome invaders like bacteria, viruses and parasites that come into our digestive system along with food and drink. A healthy microbiota also produces many other important cells that are used in the immune response.

When the bacterial layer on the gut wall is damaged through abnormal gut microbiota, there are serious consequences to the immune system. The body produces fewer immune cells and the nutrients required to support the body's entire immune system are deficient due to lack of absorption. Invaders and undigested food are able to seep through the damaged gut wall, adding to the workload of an already compromised immune system. Healthy microbiota actively synthesise various nutrients – many, like folic acid, thiamine (B1), riboflavin (B2), pyridoxine (B6) and cyanocobalamin (B12), are essential nutrients for immune function; devoid of this essential nourishment, the immune system becomes further malnourished.

Antibiotics, analgesics, steroids, stress, pollution and chemicals can all have a detrimental effect on the gut microbiota. The foods we eat have a profound impact on the composition of the bacteria living in our gut. Processed carbohydrates (especially sugar) feed pathogenic bacteria, crowding out the beneficial bacteria. Incidentally, this is why fermented foods like kefir, sauerkraut and kimchi are particularly effective at supporting good bacterial balance in the gut.

Optimum intake of Vitamin C is essential for healthy immune function. In the 1970s, Dr Linus Pauling showed that Vitamin C helped combat the common cold. As part of the same research, Dr Pauling also found that sugar severely slowed down the healing process. Vitamin C helps immune cells to mature, supports the reproduction of antibodies whose function is to stop bacteria from producing toxins and viruses from entering cells, and aids the macrophage, large, specialized cells that recognize, engulf and destroy invaders. Rosehip, blackberries and elderberries are good sources of Vitamin C in the autumn; kale, cauliflower and broccoli in the winter; raspberries, blueberries and strawberries in the summer; and nettles, parsley and asparagus in the spring.

Vitamin D is essential for a healthy immune system, as it triggers and arms the body's lymphocytes. Without adequate Vitamin D, the lymphocytes are unable to react to and fight off serious infections. Most Vitamin D is produced from the skin's exposure to sunlight; lack of sunlight will cause a deficiency, so supplementary Vitamin D will need to come from the diet. Good food sources include eggs, fatty fish and mushrooms.

Of course, no nutrient works in isolation, and a healthy immune system is dependent on a myriad of nutrients. Sourcing food grown in living soils and containing the highest possible levels of nutrients will help support the strength and vitality of the immune system.

Research by Professor Carlo Leifert of Newcastle University showed that there is a higher concentration of nutrients in organically grown food – in particular, he found considerably higher levels of some nutrients, including Vitamin C, zinc and iron, than in non-organic counterparts. Plant phytonutrients, many of them powerful antioxidants, are much higher in organically grown plants. Nitrogen-rich, artificial fertilisers get in the way of the plant producing these compounds, as do pesticides and herbicides.

Various studies have shown that many widely-used insecticides, herbicides and fungicides can alter our immune system and suppress normal immune system responses. These changes can reduce the body's normal resistance to bacterial, viral and other infections.

Allergies and food intolerances are a major strain on the immune system. If you think that you might have an allergy or food intolerance, stop eating the suspect food for three weeks, then reintroduce it slowly to see if you suffer a reaction. The main culprits are likely to be wheat and dairy products and soya; look also at your favourite foods eaten on a regular basis.

Allergens cause inflammation of the intestinal lining; this compromises digestion and reduces the ability to absorb nutrients from food. The undigested food particles leak across the inflamed and damaged intestinal wall into your blood system, triggering an immune response.

There are other factors that also influence immunity. A body constantly under stress, be it physical, mental or emotional, compromises the immune system. Stress-reducing activities such as meditation have been shown to produce positive changes in the immune system. Massage, too, has been shown to improve immune function. Regular exercise such as cycling, swimming or walking not only reduces stress, but supports the lymphatic system to remove toxins from the body. Lack of sleep will activate the stress response and depress immune function. If you are beginning to feel tired and jaded, it is worth aiming for a minimum of eight hours of sleep (at least two of these before midnight!) for your body to go through the vital regenerative processes.

Research has shown that having strong relationships boosts physical and mental health. Several studies have found that people who feel connected to friends have a stronger immune system than those who feel alone, and that laughing (and smiling) reduces stress hormones and supports the immune system.

The immune system glossary

Spleen	Positioned high on the left side of the abdomen between the stomach and the left kidney, the spleen has the largest collection of lymph tissue in the body. The spleen contains many specialised cells of the immune system and is the main organ that filters the blood.
Thymus	This small, butterfly-shaped organ sits between your breastplate and your heart. Fully developed at birth, it grows until puberty, then shrinks back to its birth size. During its most active time, the thymus is responsible for directing the maturation of T cells (lymphocytes).
Lymphatic system	The lymphatic system transports foreign substances, cancer cells and dead or damaged cells from the tissues of the body to the lymph nodes – here they are filtered out and destroyed. The lymph is then filtered and returned to the bloodstream.
Bone marrow	Lying in the interior of bones, the bone marrow is where many of the cells essential to immunity originate. Some of these cells mature in the bone marrow and some travel to other areas of the body to complete their maturation.
Antigens	Any substances not identified as part of the body that cause an immune response are called antigens.
Antibody (immunoglobulin)	An antibody is a protein produced by B cells that tightly binds to an antigen, either tagging the invader for attack or directly neutralising it.
B cell	A B cell (B lymphocyte) is a white blood cell that produces antibodies specific to the antigen that stimulated their production.

Basophil	A basophil is a white blood cell that releases histamine to attract other white blood cells to a place where they are needed.
Cytokines	Cytokines are the immune system's messengers. They help to regulate an immune response.
Eosinophil	Eosinophil is a white blood cell that kills bacteria and other foreign cells.
Helper T cell	A helper T cell is a white blood cell that helps B cells produce antibodies against antigens, helps activate killer T cells and stimulates macrophages.
Killer T cell	A killer T cell attaches to and kills infected cells and cancer cells.
Lymphocyte	The lymphocyte is the white blood cell that protects the body against foreign material. There are 2 types: T lymphocytes and B lymphocytes.
Macrophage	A macrophage is a type of white blood cell that ingests and destroys bacteria and other foreign cells.
Neutrophil	Neutrophil is another white blood cell that engulfs and kills bacteria and other foreign cells.
Phagocytosis	Phagocytosis is the process of a cell engulfing and ingesting unwanted material.
T cell	A T cell is a white blood cell that helps end an immune response.

immune-strengthening salads

SPRING

Dandelion, radish and asparagus salad

Serves 4
12 asparagus spears
2 tablespoons hemp oil
1 tablespoon lemon juice
16 dandelion leaves
2 handfuls of salad leaves
12 radishes, cut in half
handful of sprouted sunflower seeds
bunch of chervil, roughly chopped
salt and black pepper

Break off the woody ends of the asparagus and discard. Plunge the asparagus into boiling water for a minute, drain and refresh with cold water.

In a large bowl, whisk together the hemp oil and lemon juice and season well with salt and pepper. Add the dandelion leaves, salad leaves, asparagus, radish, sunflower seeds and chervil to the bowl and very gently mix together.

....

SUMMER

Tomato salad

Serves 4
6 tablespoons olive oil
1 tablespoon balsamic vinegar
1 bunch of watercress, picked over and
    roughly torn into pieces
3 handfuls of rocket
6 tomatoes, cut into quarters
handful of basil leaves, roughly torn
12 olives (without stones)
salt and pepper

In a large bowl, whisk together the olive oil and balsamic vinegar. Season well with salt and pepper. Add the salad ingredients to the dressing, mix well and serve.

AUTUMN

Roast pumpkin and broccoli salad with beetroot and hemp

Serves 4
1kg pumpkin, cut into 2cm pieces
4 tablespoons olive oil (plus 2 tablespoons for
    roasting)
1 head of broccoli, cut into florets
1 tablespoon tamari
3 medium beetroots, peeled and grated
2 cloves garlic, very finely diced
6 leaves sage, very finely shredded
1 tablespoon apple cider vinegar
1 teaspoon wholegrain mustard
1 teaspoon honey
4 handfuls of salad leaves
4 tablespoons shelled hemp seed
salt and black pepper

Preheat the oven to 220°C/425°F/Gas mark 7.

Toss the pumpkin in a tablespoon of olive oil, season with salt and pepper, place on a baking tray and roast until just golden and tender. Toss the broccoli florets in a tablespoon each of olive oil and tamari, add to the baking tray and roast the broccoli and pumpkin for a further 5 minutes – then remove from the oven.

Grate the beetroot and mix in the garlic and sage. Whisk the apple cider vinegar, remaining olive oil, mustard and honey together, and season well with salt and pepper.

Put the salad leaves in a large bowl and pile on the beetroot. Place the broccoli and butternut squash on top. Spoon over the dressing, and scatter over the hemp seeds.

Warm kale salad with shiitake mushrooms

Serves 4
4 large handfuls of kale (hard stalk
    removed), shredded
3 tablespoons olive oil
water
1 tablespoon tamari
1 teaspoon thyme, finely chopped
half a thumb-sized piece of ginger, finely
    grated
1 small chilli, finely chopped
225g shiitake mushrooms
2 sticks of celery, cut into matchsticks
2 carrots, cut into matchsticks
salt and pepper

Place the kale in a large pan with 2 tablespoons of olive oil and 2 tablespoons of water, stir well and cook for about three minutes until wilted. Add the tamari, increase the heat and cook until the liquid has evaporated. Stir in the thyme, ginger and chilli.

Cook the shiitake in a tablespoon of olive oil over a medium heat until softened and beginning to crisp. Add the shiitake, celery and carrots to the kale mixture. Season with salt and pepper. Divide between 4 bowls and serve.

rainbow foods

Eating a colourful rainbow of plants every day is hugely beneficial to our health. Vegetables and fruits are full of compounds known as phytonutrients, which are produced by plants to protect themselves against strong sunlight, oxidation, viruses, bacteria, insects, disease and background radiation. When we eat a diet rich in plants, we harness these amazing powers, and the plants' protection becomes our protection. Phytonutrients are associated with the prevention of at least three of the leading causes of death in Western countries – cancer, diabetes and cardiovascular disease. They are involved in a variety of processes including ones that help prevent cell damage, prevent cancer cells replicating, and strengthen the immune system. Many hundreds of these compounds have been discovered, but researchers presently estimate there could be up to 50,000 phytonutrients in plant life.

Phytonutrients are grouped according to their chemical structure and biological activity. These groups include terpenes, organosulfides, phenols and organic acids. Any one food can contain several different classifications of phytonutrients; broccoli and kale in particular contain a wide variety. Some of these compounds are antioxidant, some help in a particular way like protecting the eyes against macular degeneration, and others give cardiovascular protection. The level of phytonutrients in any plant is influenced by a variety of factors – for example, hybrid varieties have bred out many beneficial phytonutrients – and the condition of the soil will also make a difference to the level of phytonutrients in a plant.

Research shows that organic food has more phytonutrients than non-organic crops. This is hardly surprising when you consider the effect of chemical pesticides. Chemicals used to kill insects and other problems that might attack fruits and vegetables take away the natural protective strategy of the plant, which is to make phytonutrients to protect itself, so the phytonutrient content is reduced and, in turn, so are the health benefits to us when we eat the plant.

Carotenoids are from the terpene group. They are responsible for the red, orange and yellow colours in vegetables and fruits. There are many different carotenoids, including alpha-carotene, which is found in carrots, and lycopene, found in tomatoes and rosehips. Although you cannot see the colour because of the chlorophyll, the carotenoid beta-carotene is found in leafy green vegetables, and the powerful antioxidant carotenoid lutein is found in kale.

Organosulfides include many important compounds. Of particular importance are the indoles, found in the brassica family and mustard plants, and the thiosulfinates, found in garlic, onion, leeks, asparagus and shallots. It has been shown that these compounds protect against cancer and shrink tumours.

Blue, indigo and violet colours in vegetables and fruits like aubergine, grapes and blackberries come from their phenolic content. Health benefits of the phenol group include action against allergies and free radicals, enhancing the immune system, protecting against heart disease and slowing the ageing process.

Ellagic acid is a phytochemical found in many foods, especially apples, grapes, strawberries and, in particular, red raspberries. Research has shown that ellagic acid strongly inhibits cancerous cells, particularly in breast, pancreatic, oesophageal, skin, colon and prostate cancer.

Phytonutrients, unlike proteins, carbohydrates, fats, minerals and vitamins, are not considered essential for life, but as we learn more and more about the healing power of phytonutrients, we understand that they are essential for optimal health and longevity. Research has also shown that a combination of phytonutrients found in foods has a far greater protective effect than individual compounds, so the best way to reap the extraordinary benefits of phytonutrients is to eat a colourful rainbow of vegetables and fruit every day.

Red	Cherries, raspberries, tomatoes, red onions
Orange	Apricots, orange pepper, pumpkin, carrots
Yellow	Lemons, yellow beans, sweetcorn, grapefruit
Green	Asparagus, broccoli, salad leaves, kale
Blue	Borage flowers, blueberries, plums, damsons
Indigo	Black grapes, blackcurrants, purple peppers, elderberries
Violet	Red cabbage, red kohlrabi, aubergine, figs

Antioxidants are substances that protect the body from free radical damage. Free radicals are formed largely as a by-product of the body burning food to make energy, so they are part of our natural metabolism. They are also created by environmental factors including smoking, pesticides, pollution and radiation. Free radicals are atoms without a full outer shell of electrons. They are unstable and seek out electrons wherever they can so that they can become stable.

When a free radical attacks a molecule for its electron, the molecule in turn will become a free radical, causing a chain reaction which can result in massive destruction. Free radicals can attack and infiltrate every cell in your body. They are particularly damaging to the fats that make up our cell walls. Free radicals damage DNA, attacking the sugars and phosphates that form the backbone of the double helix and leading to mutations.

The body has antioxidant enzymes designed to deactivate free radicals before they cause damage, but our bodies invariably create more free radicals than the enzymes can handle, resulting in degeneration of the body. Antioxidants give their own electrons to the free radicals to help prevent cellular damage. Once an antioxidant has neutralised a free radical, it becomes inactive, so our body needs a continuous and bountiful supply of antioxidants. Many phytonutrients have antioxidant capabilities, especially the carotenoids. Other important antioxidants are Vitamins C and E, zinc, selenium and co-enzyme Q10.

Rainbow energy

The energy of the sun sends a rainbow of colours to the earth. These colours have a long healing tradition. One of the oldest concepts is that of healing the energies of the body through the chakras, which were first mentioned in the ancient Vedas, Hinduism's sacred writings. This tradition supports the existence of spinning wheels of light known as chakras existing within the 'subtle body' (the non-physical psychic body, beyond the physical body). Each chakra has a specific expression and resonates with a specific colour.

- The root chakra is located at the base of the spine and represents connection to the earth and the feeling of being grounded. The root chakra resonates with the colour red.

- The sacral chakra is located in the lower abdomen and is the seat of our emotions. Orange has the same vibrational frequency as the sacral chakra.

- The solar plexus chakra is in the upper abdomen and represents our ability to be confident and centred in our lives. Yellow is the colour of the solar plexus.

- The heart chakra is located at the centre of the chest just above the heart and represents our ability to love. This chakra resonates with the colour green.

- The throat chakra represents our ability to communicate and resonates with the colour blue.

- The third eye chakra is located in the forehead between the eyes and represents our ability to focus and see the bigger picture. Indigo is the colour of the third eye chakra.

- The crown chakra located at the top of the head represents our ability to be fully connected spiritually and resonates with the colour violet.

- Different coloured foods carry vibrations that can activate or help balance our chakras – another very good reason to eat rainbow foods.

healing power of plants

Food	Phytonutrient	Property
Orange peppers Carrots Apricots Butternut squash	Beta-carotene	Antioxidant and anti-inflammatory
Beetroots Blueberries Cherries Red cabbage	Anthocyanins	Antioxidant. Supports connective tissue regeneration
Strawberries Cherries Raspberries Blackberries	Ellagic acid	Prevents carcinogens from destroying cell membranes
Lemons Grapefruits Oranges Limes	Limonene	Breaks down carcinogens when they reach the liver
Cabbage Broccoli Kale Brussels	Indole-3-carbinol	Strong antioxidant. Protective against breast and cervical cancer
Cauliflower Apples Leeks Garlic	Quercetin	Anti-inflammatory and anti-allergic. Improves cardiovascular health
Tomatoes Asparagus Pink grapefruits Watermelon	Lycopene	A very efficient antioxidant. Protective against prostate cancer
Blueberries Mulberries Bilberries Grapes	Resveratrol	Protects skin cells. Protects the heart
Red peppers Spinach Collards Kale	Lutein	Lowers the risk of age-related vision loss. Reduces risk of artery disease
Shiitake mushrooms	Lentinan	Boosts immune function and prevents growth of cancer cells

taste

Sweet, sour, salty and bitter – these are the four tastes we generally think about when we consider taste. However, there is a distinct fifth taste, known as umami. A Japanese chemist, Kikunae Ikeda, was responsible for discovering the umami taste. Probably the best way of describing this taste is deliciously savoury. It was in the deep, rich, deliciously savoury dashi stock used in Japanese cooking and made using the sea vegetable kombu that Ikeda first identified the flavour umami, which comes from the amino acid glutamate. Delighted with his discovery, he seized his chance and went on to manufacture industrial quantities and patent the notorious monosodium glutamate (MSG) as a flavour enhancer.

In traditional Chinese medicine there are five tastes, not only sweet, sour, salty and bitter, but also pungent. Each taste acts on a specific organ more than others. The sour flavour is most closely associated with the liver, the sweet flavour with the spleen, the salty flavour with the kidney, the bitter flavour the heart and the pungent flavour with the lungs.

Our fascination with taste has led the French to recently discover a specific fat taste and the Japanese to announce the discovery of a 'hearty' new taste, kokumi, which doesn't seem to have its own specific flavour but enhances the flavours with which it's combined.

So what is the purpose of taste? Of course, it brings immense pleasure – though one could argue it can bring displeasure as well! People experience taste in different ways depending on the number of taste buds on the tongue. Some people are particularly sensitive to taste and are known as super tasters, and they are often employed in the food industry to taste new products. It is mistakenly thought that we taste different flavours on different parts of the tongue, but, actually, each taste bud recognises every taste. In the blink of an eye, up to 10,000 taste buds evaluate millions of molecules in the food you eat. Taste is also cultural – what tastes sublime to one culture may not be so acceptable to another. Strawberries and cream on a summer's day may seem delightful to us, whereas, in general, seal blubber ice cream (akutaq) from Alaska may not.

From an evolutionary perspective, taste is how our ancestors decided what was good to eat. The sweet taste signified energy-dense food, particularly important if you were unsure where your next meal was coming from. The bitter taste generally enabled harmful substances to be avoided, the salty taste may have been part of an evolutionary process that helped us control sodium levels in the body, and it is suggested that the sour taste enabled us to avoid digesting too many acids, possibly from unripe fruits or deteriorating foods. Our modern food industry tricks our taste buds by manipulating the taste of food and encouraging us to eat unhealthy food. By eating food from healthy soils teeming with life, freshly prepared or preserved using artisan tradition, we honour (and excite) our taste buds.

fermenting

Fermented foods have evolved through mutual relationships: microorganisms need a substrate on which to feed and the incidental fermented foods that are made are both delicious and beneficial for us to eat. Bacteria were the first inhabitants on Earth, and continuously for two billion years they transformed the planet's surface. Lynn Margulis, a biologist whose work on the origin of cells helped transform the study of evolution, showed how the essential processes of life evolved because of bacteria and that planet Earth is made fertile and inhabitable for larger life forms by a worldwide system of communicating, gene-exchanging bacteria. When we harness the power of bacteria with the art of fermentation, we are connected to our earliest beginnings.

In general, we seem to have been indoctrinated into destroying bacteria. We sterilise our hands, our bodies, our homes and our food. Of course, some bacteria do cause disease, but the overwhelming majority help prevent it. Herbalist and healer Stephen Harrod Buhner emphasises that bacteria are not our enemies, but rather they play an integral role in supporting, maintaining and rebuilding health: 'In declaring war on bacteria, we declared war on the underlying living structure of the planet; on all life-forms we can see; on ourselves.'

Fermentation, until relatively recently, was a process steeped in mystery, but the extraordinary transformations were welcomed as very desirable foods. Most ferments are activated by bacteria, yeasts and moulds, often working together to create unforgettable flavours including sauerkraut, kimchi, umeboshi, tempeh, miso, tamari, cacao nibs, capers, olives, vinegar, wine, yoghurt, kefir and cheese. The *Lactobacillus* species is the most prolific bacteria responsible for fermented dairy and vegetables. The most familiar yeast in fermenting is *Saccharomyces cerevisiae*, which has been used in brewing and baking for thousands of years. The main mould used, predominantly in Asian products, is *Aspergillus oryzae*.

Records of fermenting date back as far as 6000BC to the fertile crescent of the Middle East, and nearly every civilisation since that time has harnessed the transforming abilities of microorganisms to improve, preserve and protect their food. Kvass (a sour bread drink) from Russia, kiviaq (preserved sea birds) from Greenland, douchi (fermented soybeans) from China, amazake (a sweet rice pudding

drink) from Japan, beirta (goat meat) from the Sudan, mam (seafood) from Vietnam and surströmming (fermented herring) from Sweden demonstrate how cultures from around the globe have created a myriad of unique flavours and traditions around fermentation. Traditionally, in cold climates fermentation was an essential survival strategy. In the summer months when the ice melted, people caught fish and birds, which they buried in pits and left to ferment until the winter months when food was scarce. In hot tropical countries, fermentation made sure food was transformed into something delicious rather than allowing the tropical heat to decompose the food and make it inedible.

'In declaring war on bacteria, we declared war on the underlying living structure of the planet; on all life-forms we can see; on ourselves.' – Stephen Harrod Buhner

Lactic acid fermentation of vegetables is one of the easiest to experiment with at home. By submerging vegetables under liquid, you create an environment where anaerobic-loving lactic acid bacteria, mainly *Lactobacillus* species, convert sugar into lactic acid, a natural preservative. Salt plays an important role, creating conditions that favour the bacteria, preventing the growth of undesirable microorganisms, pulling water from the vegetables and adding flavour. Everyone develops their own fermentation practice and there are endless variations to experiment with. It doesn't take long to understand what works for you – develop your own rhythm and create an endless variety of ferments.

Cereal grains, corn, wheat, rice, barley, sorghum, millet, rye and oats are grown and eaten in vast quantities across the world. Traditional culinary practices ferment these grains, making them far easier to digest. In Africa, a porridge known as ogi is made out of fermented millet; in India, rice and lentils are fermented for a couple of days before making idli and dosas. Corn was always fermented before use in Mexico, and throughout Europe grains were soaked overnight in soured milk to make porridge in the morning. It's very easy to start soaking grains, and this simple process is an enormous aid to digestion. Simply soak your chosen grain in water for a minimum of eight hours at room temperature; you can assist the process by adding a little fermented vegetable juice or yoghurt.

Beans can also be difficult to digest, and the fermenting process transforms them into a far more digestible food. Tempeh is relatively easy to make, and freshly made tempeh is incomparable to anything that you buy. Tempeh is traditionally made by growing moulds – predominantly *Rhizopus oligosporus* – on cooked soya beans, though actually it works with any beans or a mixture of beans and grains.

It's not too difficult to make your own tempeh; it requires only a few ingredients: cooked beans, tempeh starter and vinegar. The hardest part is the incubation period; it needs to be kept at a temperature of between 29–32°C for about 24 hours, so you will need to create some kind of incubation chamber (a dehydrator, if you have one, works really well). Once you master the art, you will be rewarded with a firm, easy-to-digest, protein-rich food, high in beneficial nutrition and fibre.

The traditional ferment of miso is made by mixing cooked, crushed soya beans, koji, salt and water. Sweet miso is left to ferment for 6–8 weeks; darker, salty miso is left for between 6–12 months. Koji is made from steamed pearled barley or lightly milled rice impregnated with *Aspergillus oryzae* spores.

Different types of koji and varying proportions of ingredients used in a recipe create a wide range of misos, from light and sweet to dark and robust. Miso has long been considered a potent medicine in the East. The long-fermented varieties are especially high in easy-to-assimilate nutrients; in addition, miso contains the plant isoflavone genistein, which is a potent anti-cancer agent, as well as dipicolinic acid, an alkaloid that chelates heavy metals and discharges them from the body. Sandor Katz talks you through making miso in the book *Wild Fermentation*. It takes time, and even if you start today you will have to wait months before it is ready, so in the meantime seek out some unpasteurised misos to buy.

Generally, making your own ferments is easy, especially lactic fermented vegetables, and before long you will be creating an infinite variety of combinations and flavours and reaping the benefits.

the benefits of fermented foods

Fermentation preserves food
Alcohol, lactic acid and acetic acid produced by fermenting organisms all prevent spoilage and preserve nutrients.

Fermentation breaks down food to make digestion and assimilation easier
Protein-rich soya beans, for example, are largely indigestible without fermentation.

Fermentation creates new nutrients
Microbial cultures create B vitamins, particularly thiamine, niacin, riboflavin, biotin and folic acid.

Fermentation removes toxins from food
Fermentation can reduce naturally occurring toxins in some foods, making them safe to eat. Cassava, long eaten in Africa, has semi-dangerous levels of cyanide, which is eliminated when the cassava is fermented.

Fermentation is more energy efficient
Fermentation reduces the need for both cooking and refrigeration, so it is more energy efficient.

Fermented foods contain higher levels of convertible energy
They often contain a higher level of convertible energy than non-fermented foods of the same weight.

Fermented foods are beneficial for people with diabetes
The carbohydrates in lactic acid-fermented foods have been broken down or 'pre-digested'. As a result, they do not place an extra burden on the pancreas, unlike ordinary carbohydrates.

Raw lacto-fermented food and drink introduces beneficial bacteria into your gut
They introduce beneficial bacteria into your digestive system.

Fermented foods nourish beneficial gut bacteria
They are prebiotic, providing the right food for the beneficial gut bacteria.

Fermented foods support better absorption of nutrients
By supporting gut bacteria balance and providing digestive enzymes, fermented foods help you to absorb more of the nutrients from your food.

Fermented foods support the function of the immune system
A healthy gut microbiota through eating fermented foods supports the immune system.

Fermented foods taste delicious
Fermented foods add complex and delicious flavours to meals.

Tempeh

500g peas/beans
2½ tablespoons vinegar
1½ teaspoons tempeh starter

Soak beans in water overnight.

Cook them the next morning, keeping them slightly underdone. Strain and gently pat dry with a towel. Place in food processor and pulse to break up, but keep some whole so there is texture, and place in a bowl. Alternatively, place the beans in a bowl and crush with a flat-ended rolling pin. Let cool to body temperature.

Add vinegar and mix well. Add the tempeh starter and mix thoroughly. Place into 2 small zip-lock plastic bags (approx. 180 x 220mm) that you have poked holes in with a fork. Incubate for about 24 hours at about 29–32°C. Keep an eye on the temperature, as the process generates its own heat. A cohesive mat will form, and eventually patches of grey will appear near the holes.

Remove from the incubator, cool to room temperature, then refrigerate or freeze.

The best material for culturing is not plastic, but it's hard to know what other material to use. In Indonesia banana leaves are used to wrap the tempeh during incubation time. A mulberry leaf or large vine leaf would work, but it's probably best to get the hang of the process with the bag first.

food and community

Sharing food, with all its traditions, customs and social implications, plays an essential role in building community. When our only source of food came from hunting and gathering, we were drawn together to find food by working cooperatively – a group of hunters was far more likely to make a successful kill than a lone one. Hunted animals and wild-gathered plants were brought back to the homestead and shared communally. Sharing food supported the development of language, experiences and skills. Tracking, hunting, gathering, fishing and all forms of foraging require an intimate knowledge of the environment and the nature of the food being sought, establishing a deep understanding and respect of the interconnectedness of life on Earth and the importance of community.

About 10,000 years ago this way of living, which required constantly moving about the land, began to be replaced by settlements; as they grew, so did the emergence of agriculture, and our diet became less dependent on the cooperation and skills needed to provide food from the wild. Today, in the West, technological developments in agriculture have led to a disconnection between soil, food and communities living together around food.

Indigenous people have unique food cultures and customs that are built on an intimate relationship with the land. Communities flourish through a keen knowledge of how to eat nutritiously without damaging the ecosystem. For many indigenous peoples, their food systems are self-sufficient and their way of life around food builds strong thriving communities.

Whilst traditional foods and dietary diversity within an ecosystem can be a powerful source of nutrients and good health for the indigenous peoples of the world, there are those who are vulnerable to lack of food. Globalisation and environmental degradation have far-reaching effects on the food systems of indigenous people; it is imperative to conserve ecosystems that contain the food resources necessary for their community health. It is well documented that the introduction of processed foods, refined fats and oils, and simple carbohydrates contributes to a massive decline in the health of indigenous people.

Today in the West there is a growing movement to reconnect to the land: more and more people are remembering how meaningful

growing, cooking and sharing food can be. By being involved in a
community of family, friends, neighbours or colleagues, we develop
a strong sense of caring for each other. Sharing food around the
table brings an opportunity to build on these relationships and
strengthen community ties. This is where we listen to stories, grow
creative ideas and connect more deeply to each other.

seven flavours of autumn

Blackberry
Blackberries must be the best-known wild-gathered berry. Of course, there are plenty of cultivated ones now available, but there is a far greater sense of satisfaction if you pick your own in the dappled autumn sun and return home with stained hands and lips. Blackberries are a good source of Vitamin C and provide a fair amount of iron. The blackberry leaf and root are powerful astringents and the berries are used to treat diarrhoea and anaemia.

Figs
Figs originated in Southwest Asia, and they now grow throughout the Mediterranean and surprisingly well in Britain. The medicinal use of figs is almost as ancient as the plant itself. For centuries, figs have been recommended to restore energy and vitality. Pliny wrote, 'Figs are restorative and the best food that can be taken by those who are brought low by a long sickness'. They can be turned into a variety of dishes, but frankly they are delicious just the way they are.

Elderberry
Elderberries are another autumn fruit dripping from the tree to gather by the basket. Elderberry vinegar added to warm water makes a delicious healthy winter drink. They strengthen the immune system and reduce the severity and duration of colds and flu. Elderberries are a rich source of Vitamins A, B and C, potassium and antioxidants. Some research suggests they may be better than blueberries at fighting free radicals.

Fennel seed
Fennel seeds are one of the nine sacred Anglo Saxon herbs symbolising longevity, courage and strength. I love the fresh green seeds before they are dried; they add an aromatic burst of flavour to food. Fennel seeds are a potent medicine containing loads of minerals and vitamins including copper, iron, zinc, calcium and Vitamins A, E and C plus B complex. They have long been used as a remedy for indigestion and relief of colic pain in newborn babies.

Apple

Fresh-picked apples are one of the evocative smells of autumn. Many apples, kept in a dry room, will keep into the following year. Apples are packed with disease-fighting vitamins and antioxidants. Juicing apples from time to time is fine, but eating them in their whole form will give you a synergistic blend of nutrients and fibre the way nature intended, providing you with well-researched health benefits.

Pumpkin

There are many different varieties of pumpkins: some are tiny and nestle in the palm of your hand, others are too big to move single-handed. Halloween jack-o'-lanterns make pumpkins synonymous with autumn. All the scooped-out flesh can be turned into endless dishes, from soups and risotto to muffins and pies. The fruit is a good source of Vitamin B complex as well as many antioxidant vitamins such as A, C and E. Pumpkin is also a rich source of minerals like copper, calcium, potassium and phosphorus.

Rosehip

Like jewels, rosehips cascade down the bushes in the autumn. These oval, red fruits of wild roses have long been used as food and medicine. Turn them into chutneys, jams, syrups, vinegars, wine and teas. Rosehip tea was traditionally used for the common cold and locally for inflamed or bleeding gums. During the Second World War, many tonnes of rosehips were turned into syrup to provide Vitamin C.

revitalising ritual, every day, every mouthful

Miche Fabre Lewin

I cook on a Zen meditation retreat in Wales. At every meal we all repeat a grace before eating...

> 'At one with the food we eat, we identify with the universe;
> At one with the universe, we taste the food.
> The universe and the food we eat partake of the same nature.'

Then we sit in silence to share the plant-based meal, which has been prepared from organic vegetables and artisan condiments. During this time of reflective silence, eating becomes a practice in mindfulness. With every slowly chewed mouthful I inhabit the present moment and feel my connection with the spirit of nature. This retreat is my own sanctuary and brings me peace and deep joy.

Rituals and ceremonies with food tell stories. Convivial celebrations with food are times for nurturing our relationships with each other. Through food we taste our history, we remember our cultural connections, we celebrate our origins in nature, we prepare for the future.

Around the world we enter into rituals with food through anniversaries, festivals, celebrations and religious rites. Food rituals offer sensuous and collective experiences whereby we can reconnect and honour our place within the ecosystem.

In the ancient worlds there are many thanksgiving traditions based around food, and the gods were honoured and appeased by food offerings. Within our contemporary cultures in Britain, ceremonies which honour our relationship to the earth are evident during harvest time, with thanksgiving rituals appreciating the bounty of nature. The First Fruits ceremony in South Africa is a celebration of the new season's crops, first enjoyed by the chiefs, and as a food ritual, it serves as a way of bringing individuals together in community. In biodynamic agriculture, there are seasonal song rituals, which invite the audience to sing to the farm animals as a blessing and thanksgiving for what they bring to our lives.

Food has the potential to keep us in a continuous exchange with the cycles of nature, and it has a symbolic role within agricultural and culinary traditions. During the Jewish Passover Seder, a ritual plate, laid on the table and containing six foods with symbolic meaning, tells the story of the ancient Hebrew exodus from Egypt. Among these foods, horseradish recalls the bitter suffering, the roasted egg represents renewal, and the salted water symbolises the tears and sweat of enslavement. In Christian traditions, the Holy Communion uses food as a symbol for the body of Christ – the wine is his blood and the wafer biscuit is his body. These are tasted and drunk to remember, through our own bodies, our relationship to the sacred.

How can we introduce simple and meaningful ways of food making that connect us to the earth? Find a local farm shop. Become a member of a community-supported farm. Join a weekly vegetable box scheme. These relationships make for a good food experience and give meaning to the cooking, preparing and sharing of a meal. Begin to compost your food to make food for the earth. Start growing herbs and vegetables. These are direct ways of remembering our interconnectedness with nature.

Every day, every mouthful, we can celebrate that we are part of the cycle of life and honour that we are born out of soil, that we share in nature's bounty, that Earth is our mother. Feeding ourselves with vital food to nourish the body is an act of generosity for ourselves, our families, our communities and the planet.

The simple action of lighting a candle as we sit down to eat is one which brings recognition, respect and a sense of harmony. It invites a space to pause, to reflect, to thank and to celebrate.

Rituals of the Kitchen
Look into your food cupboards – empty, clean, clear, refresh. Make space to cook.

Rituals of the Table
Put food into beautiful vessels – light a candle, chew food slowly, leave time to sit and digest.

Rituals of the Land
Remember and honour our relationship with soil through composting, blessing seeds, showing gratitude to plants and singing to animals.

First know food.
From food all things are born.
By food they live,
Towards food they move,
And into food they return.

In knowing food we come to know ourselves and discover ways of living well with ourselves, each other and the planet.

Miche Fabre Lewin is an ecological artist who has an ever-evolving body of healing work that is performative, participatory and rooted in soil, food and ritual.

autumn recipes

Blackberry and apple juice
Green pepper, tomato, celery, garlic and
horseradish juice
Fig and chocolate smoothie Ⓝ
Apple granola Ⓝ
Frisée, watercress and radicchio with Russet
apples and walnuts Ⓝ
Garden salad leaves with fig balsamic dressing
Red and yellow tomato soups with chive oil
Baked butternut squash with spiced quinoa
stuffing and roast red pepper dressing
Potato, spinach and fava beans with coriander
Sourdough rye bread Ⓖ
Sauerkraut
Kimchi
Rosehip chutney
Carrot cake with hemp cream Ⓔ Ⓝ
Chocolate mousse Ⓝ
Spiced elderberry syrup
Blackberry vinegar

Ⓖ *– contains gluten*
Ⓓ *– contains dairy*
Ⓢ *– contains soya*
Ⓔ *– contains eggs*
Ⓝ *– contains nuts*

Blackberry and apple juice

Serves 1
3 apples (use up windfalls)
a couple of handfuls of blackberries
1 slice of lemon (with skin)

Cut up the apples, but do not core or peel. If they are windfalls, remove any bruised bits.

Put all the ingredients through a juicer. If you use cooking apples, you might like to add half a teaspoon of raw honey. Drink at once – taste the season!

....

Green pepper, tomato, celery, garlic and horseradish juice

Serves 1
6 ripe vine tomatoes
1 small green jalapeño pepper
2 sticks of celery
1 clove garlic
half a thumb-sized piece of horseradish root,
    scrubbed and peeled

Juice all the ingredients for an amazing, immune-boosting drink.

....

Fig and chocolate smoothie ⓝ

Serves 1
4 fresh figs (hard tip removed)
1 pear, quartered and cored
115ml almond milk
1 tablespoon raw cacao powder

Put all the ingredients in a blender and blend until the mixture is smooth. Pour into a glass and drink.

Apple granola

175g apple purée (made from Bramleys
 lightly cooked until pulpy – keep as
 dry as possible)
50g date paste
2 tablespoons maple syrup
1 teaspoon vanilla essence
½ teaspoon cinnamon powder
2 tablespoons sunflower seeds, soaked
2 tablespoons pumpkin seeds, soaked
200g mixed dried fruit and nuts, chopped
 (anything you have in the cupboard will
 do, but a good combination would be 75g
 chopped almonds, 75g chopped walnuts,
 50g dried sour cherries)

In the food processor, blend the apple purée, date paste, maple
syrup, vanilla essence and cinnamon. Add the sunflower and
pumpkin seeds, and pulse until coarsely chopped. Transfer to a bowl.
 Add the remaining ingredients, mix well, then spread thinly
on dehydrator trays lined with baking paper or dehydrator sheets.
Dry overnight set at 45°C. Peel off the paper, flip over and dry for a
further 6 hours. Break into small pieces and store in an airtight jar.

Frisée, watercress and radicchio with Russet apples and walnuts Ⓝ

Serves 4
1 head frisée
1 bunch watercress
1 radicchio
a splash of olive oil
110ml walnut oil
1 tablespoon cider vinegar
1 shallot, finely chopped
2 medium Russet apples
75g walnut pieces
salt and pepper

Carefully pick over, wash and dry the frisée and watercress. Separate the radicchio leaves and tear into pieces. Put the salad leaves in the fridge until you need them. Make the dressing by combining the oil, vinegar, and shallot, and season with salt and pepper.

Quarter and core the apples and cut into fine slices. Put into a bowl with the salad leaves and walnuts, gently toss with the dressing and serve.

....

Garden salad leaves with fig balsamic dressing

Serves 4
6 large handfuls of salad leaves
10 figs, soaked (keep the soaking water)
30ml balsamic vinegar
175ml olive oil
¼ small fresh chilli
½ teaspoon salt
1 teaspoon lemon juice
¼ teaspoon black pepper

Pick over the salad leaves and place in a large bowl. Blend the remaining ingredients together until smooth, adding the soaking water from the figs if necessary. Toss through the leaves and serve.

Red and yellow tomato soups with chive oil

Serves 4

Red

1 red onion, thinly sliced
1 tablespoon olive oil
8 deep red, vine-ripened tomatoes, roughly
    chopped
½ teaspoon sea salt
1 small chilli, finely chopped
275ml vegetable stock

In a pan, cook the onions in the olive oil over low heat until tender. Add the tomatoes, salt, chilli and stock. Bring to the boil and simmer for about 10 minutes. Cool slightly, then blend in a blender until smooth. Return to rinsed-out pan.

Yellow

1 white onion, thinly sliced
1 tablespoon olive oil
8 golden yellow tomatoes, roughly chopped
½ teaspoon sea salt
1 tablespoon marjoram leaves
275ml vegetable stock

In a pan, cook the onions in the olive oil over a low heat until tender. Add the tomatoes, salt, marjoram and stock. Bring to the boil and simmer for about 5 minutes. Cool slightly, then blend in a blender until smooth. Return to the rinsed-out pan.

Chive oil

1 handful of chives, very finely chopped
6 tablespoons olive oil
1 tablespoon lemon juice
salt and pepper to taste

Blend all the ingredients until very smooth, check for seasoning and pour into a jug.

Gently heat the soups, then, with a pan in each hand (or decanted into separate jugs), pour steadily into soup bowls so half is yellow and half is red. Finish with a dash of chive oil.

Baked butternut squash with spiced quinoa stuffing and a roast red pepper dressing

Serves 6

3 butternut squashes – big enough to serve
    half a squash to each person
350g quinoa
2 red onions, finely chopped
3 tablespoons olive oil
3 cloves garlic, finely chopped
150g shiitake mushrooms, sliced
2 celery stalks, finely chopped
½ teaspoon cumin
½ teaspoon coriander
¼ teaspoon paprika
zest of 1 lemon
2 tablespoons fresh coriander, chopped
salt and pepper

Cut the butternut squashes in half lengthways and remove the seeds. Season the insides with salt, black pepper and cumin and place cut side down on an oiled baking tray. Bake for about 20 minutes in a moderately hot oven (around 200°C) or until tender.

Rinse the quinoa in cold water, cook for approximately 12 minutes or until just cooked, strain, and set aside.

Gently cook the onions in the olive oil until beginning to soften. Add the garlic, then the shiitake mushrooms and allow the onions, garlic and mushrooms to begin to turn golden. Add the celery and cook for a further minute. Add the cumin, coriander and paprika and cook for a further 30 seconds. Remove from the heat and stir in the lemon zest and quinoa.

Gently remove most of the butternut squash from its skin and mix into the quinoa mixture. Season to taste with salt and pepper.

Fill the squash shells with the quinoa mixture, warm through in the oven, then place each one on a plate. Top with chopped coriander and spoon a generous amount of roast red pepper dressing on the side.

Red pepper dressing

3 red peppers
2 tablespoons vegetable stock
¼ teaspoon smoked paprika
a good pinch of salt

Cut the peppers in half and remove the seeds, put on a tray and blister the skins in a hot oven or under the grill until they are charred and the flesh has softened. Pop them into a lidded container until they have cooled down. Peel off the skins and purée the peppers with the stock, smoked paprika and salt until smooth.

Potato, spinach and fava beans with coriander

Serves 6
2 small onions, finely chopped
2 tablespoons olive oil
2 tablespoons water
2 teaspoons cumin seeds
½ teaspoon turmeric
5 garlic cloves, crushed
1.35kg potatoes, peeled and cut into 1/2cm dice
2 dried red chillis, crumbled
salt
450g tender spinach leaves, washed
450g cooked fava beans

Cook the onion gently in the oil with the water for 4–5 minutes, until it begins to soften and the water has evaporated. Add the cumin seeds, turmeric and garlic and cook for a further 2–3 minutes.

Add the potatoes, crumbled chilli and a little salt to taste. Stir well, then cover and cook gently for 7–8 minutes until the potatoes are tender. Add the spinach and fava beans and cook gently until heated through. Check the seasoning and serve.

Sourdough rye bread ⓖ

<u>Rye sourdough starter:</u>

DAY I
8 tablespoons filtered water, approx. 20°C
6 tablespoons rye flour
2 tablespoons raisins (optional)
Mix all ingredients together in a Kilner jar, adding more water if necessary to make a thin paste-like consistency. Cover with muslin to keep out flies, but allow the free circulation of air and leave at room temperature – approx. 20°C.

DAY 2
Add the following:
2 tablespoons water, 20°C
1 tablespoon rye flour

Stir vigorously and leave again.

DAY 3
Repeat day 2.

DAY 4
By now, you should notice bubbles on the surface of the batter – but
do not worry if this has not happened, it may just be slow.
Repeat day 2.

DAY 5
100g rye flour

Strain out the raisins if using, discard half of the batter and return
the remainder to the Kilner jar. Stir in 100g rye flour and enough
water to make a thick batter.

DAY 6
100g rye flour

By now, the fermentation should be clearly evident.
Repeat day 5.

DAY 7
Start using. Feed your leaven, after you have used it, with rye flour
and water.

Bread is about texture, consistency and trusting your intuition
rather than measurements, but here is the method:

1 part rye leaven to 1 part rye flour
salt
water
molasses
oiled tin(s), sprinkled with coriander
    or caraway seeds

Combine the ingredients together to form a soft, slightly sticky
mixture. With wet hands, shape the dough into a loaf or loaves and
place in the prepared tin(s). Flatten and press the dough down well
in the tins, sprinkle over rye flour, cover well and leave in a warm
place for about 5 hours or overnight in a cooler place until double
the size.
    Bake in a preheated oven, 220°C /425°F/Gas mark 7, for about 45
mins. Turn out onto a wire rack and cool.

Sauerkraut

3 medium white cabbage heads
sea salt
1 large, clean glass jar

Shred the cabbage and place in a large, metal bowl. Sprinkle over 2 tablespoons of salt and pound with a wooden rolling pin until the juices starts to flow. Cover with a cloth and leave overnight.

The next morning, place about 5cm of cabbage into the glass jar and press down firmly. Sprinkle with a little salt and repeat until the jar is full.

Firmly compress the layers of cabbage, leaving some space at the top of the jar because the cabbage will expand slightly as it ferments. Press the cabbage down with a jam jar filled with water or an alternative weight to make sure the cabbage is covered with liquid. Every day, push the cabbage gently down to ensure it remains under the liquid.

Let the jar sit at room temperature. After about 10 days, the cabbage will have fermented sufficiently to be eaten, but you can leave it for a further 2–3 weeks before fitting a lid and storing.

The longer it keeps, the stronger it becomes. Experiment to find the right strength for you. Store in a cool, dry place – once you start eating the fermented cabbage, keep it in the fridge.

Kimchi

1 litre brine made from 1 litre water and 4
    tablespoons salt

For the vegetables
3 turnips
3 carrots
3 Jerusalem artichokes
a few radishes (optional)

For the spices
3 tablespoons fresh ginger root, grated
4 cloves garlic, chopped
6 shallots, chopped
2 chillies, chopped whole or
    with seeds removed

Finely slice the vegetables and leave in brine overnight.

Blend spices together into a paste. Drain brine off vegetables, reserving brine. Taste them for saltiness. You want them to taste salty, but not unpleasantly so. If they are too salty, rinse them. If you cannot taste salt, sprinkle with a bit more.

Layer a couple of centimetres of vegetables into a litre jar, then add a little of the spice mixture, cover with another layer of sliced vegetables and press down tightly to encourage the brine to rise. Repeat the layering until the jar is filled. Add some of the vegetable soak water to ensure the vegetables are under liquid. Weigh down and ferment in a warm place for a week.

Rosehip chutney

550ml fresh rosehips, halved and seeds
    removed
200g raisins or sultanas
700g cooking apples, peeled, cored and
    chopped
550ml cider vinegar or wine vinegar
knob of ginger, grated
1 teaspoon cayenne pepper
1 teaspoon ground cloves
2 cloves garlic, chopped
225g demerara sugar
juice and zest of 1 lemon
juice and zest of 1 orange

Soak the rosehips, raisins or sultanas, and apples in vinegar
overnight. After soaking, place the rosehips with remaining
ingredients in a large, heavy saucepan. Bring the mixture to the boil,
then reduce heat and simmer, stirring occasionally, until mixture is
thickened. Leave to cool, then place chutney in clean, dry jars. Store
chutney in a cool place. Keep for at least a month before using.

Carrot cake with hemp cream Ⓔ Ⓝ

Serves 10
For the carrot cake
150g blanched almonds
150g rice flour
350g carrots
2 teaspoons vanilla essence
1 heaped teaspoon ground cinnamon
3 eggs
220g rapadura sugar
110g prunes, soaked
110ml olive oil

For the hemp cream
110g shelled hemp seeds
110ml water
1 teaspoon vanilla essence

Lightly oil a 20cm cake tin and line with baking paper. Heat oven to 170°C/325°F/Gas mark 3.

<u>To make the carrot cake:</u>
Process the almonds in a food processor until well ground and grate the carrots on the fine side of a grater. Place the almonds and carrots in a large mixing bowl and add the rice flour, vanilla essence and cinnamon.

Whisk the eggs together with the sugar until the mixture turns pale and becomes thick. Use the processor to whizz the prunes with the olive oil until you have a thick purée.

Stir the prune purée into the carrot and almond mixture and finally fold in the eggs and sugar.

Pour into the prepared tin and bake in the oven for about an hour, lowering to 150°C after 15 minutes. When the cake is firm to the touch, remove from the oven, allow to cool for 5 minutes, then turn out onto a cooling tray. Serve with hemp cream.

<u>To make the hemp cream:</u>
Process the seeds, water and vanilla essence in a food processor until smooth and thick.

Chocolate mousse Ⓝ

Serves 8 (small servings)
110g cashews, soaked for 12 hours and strained
6 dates, soaked
2 tablespoons raw cacao powder
1 teaspoon vanilla essence
¼ teaspoon cinnamon
8 bay leaves

Blend all together until creamy, divide between 8 shot glasses and chill. Pop a bay leaf on each one before serving.

....

Spiced elderberry syrup

1.5kg destemmed elderberries
120ml water
demerara sugar
10 cloves
½ teaspoon cinnamon powder
2 1/2cm horseradish root, grated
zest of 1 lemon

Pour the elderberries into a large pot and mash them with a potato masher. Add 110ml water and bring to the boil, stirring frequently, then simmer very gently for half an hour. Remove from the heat, cool slightly, then pour the berries into a jelly bag suspended over a large bowl. Let this drain overnight. You should have about 1.2 litres of liquid.

Return the juice to the cleaned pan, and for every 600ml of juice add 450g sugar. Add the spices and bring to the boil before reducing the heat and simmering very gently for half an hour. Pour into small, hot sterilised bottles and cover tightly. The bottles will keep for a year in a cool, dry place. Once opened, keep in the fridge.

Blackberry vinegar

Vinegar's acidity makes it an effective solvent and preservative for extracting flavours and phytochemicals from fruits and herbs.

blackberries
apple cider vinegar

Fill a jar with just-picked blackberries, cover with the vinegar and leave to infuse in a cool, dark place for a month. Strain and bottle.

winter

growing food

Our earliest ancestors were hunter-gatherers who had an intimate relationship with the land that was the source of their food; they did not take their meals for granted, and through cultural appreciation they acknowledged food as sacred. It must have been hard to know where their next meal might be coming from, and it is unlikely that meals were eaten on a regular basis, maybe not even daily, so every hard-won morsel was exceedingly precious.

About 6,500 years ago, the first farmers in Britain started clearing the native wildwood, growing crops and domesticating animals. The early days of subsistence farming slowly changed and by the 18th century agriculture was committed to increased output and greater security of supply.

Today, the predominant farming system in Britain uses large machinery, and there are far fewer people working on the land. Biodiversity of crops has greatly diminished, genetically modified organisms have been introduced, plants are subjected to synthetic pesticides and artificial fertilisers are spread on the soil. Farming has become an 'industry' rather than a 'culture', and with this shift we have lost the understanding that our food is sacred. Industrial agriculture has had a detrimental impact on rural communities, the environment and animal health.

Whatever way you look at it, animals raised for food are being treated as a means to a human end and not an end in themselves. This gives us total responsibility for their welfare, meaning we have to provide the best possible living conditions, which includes creating an environment that allows animals to maintain social structures best suited to their particular species, minimising pain and fear, and feeding animals a natural diet.

Chickens are natural omnivores that have evolved to eat insects, grubs, seeds and worms. Chickens that are allowed to roam freely outside will strut over the ground unearthing food using their powerful feet, rest in the shade of a tree and bathe in dust. A small flock of around a hundred birds is able to organise a social structure and live without undue stress.

Intensively farmed chickens reared for meat can be housed in flocks of up to 40,000. They are slaughtered at six weeks, though their natural life span can reach around ten years.

The original chicken battery cage system is banned in the EU, so industrial egg-laying chickens are kept in what is known as enriched cages, housing tens of thousands of birds. These cages are only slightly larger, and the hens remain severely restricted with no room to stretch and flap their wings. There are around 30 million hens in the UK egg-laying flock, and just over 60% are currently in cages. Around 40 million male chicks of the egg-laying breed are killed at birth each year; unable to lay eggs, and a different breed to chickens raised for meat, they are deemed of no use.

Eggs labelled 'barn' are laid by hens who are not caged, but they are confined to large barns with artificial lighting. Each barn houses up to 16,000 birds who will never see daylight or breathe fresh air. Free-range hens are often kept in 'barn'-type sheds in similar-sized flocks; they have access to the outside, but the reality is that few are likely to pick their way through the flock to reach the doors that take them to the fresh air. Most egg-laying hens, when their egg production drops, are slaughtered, normally at around 72 weeks. Their carcasses are used in cheap, processed foods such as chicken soups, pastes, pies and pet food.

The natural habitat of ducks is wetlands, ponds, rivers, lakes and oceans. Wild ducks take off from the water, fly and land back with extraordinary precision.

Farmed ducks have been bred so that their bodies are too heavy and their wings too small to support flying. Most farmed ducks are grown for market in a similar fashion to that of broiler chickens. They have been bred to grow rapidly, from hatching to slaughter in six weeks and not a pond in sight. Lack of water means factory ducks are unable to keep themselves clean and are prone to eye infections. Deprived of their natural habitat, they are unable to feed on plants, insects, worms and planktonic organisms, which form their natural diet – instead they are fed wheat-based pellets.

Pigs, as part of small-scale farming, forage, using their snouts, in the fields and woods for acorns, grubs and roots, and they give birth in straw-strewn pigsties.

Sows on industrial pig farms are kept in barns and give birth on concrete-floored pens, in very confined spaces. The piglets are weaned at four weeks and slaughtered at six months, having spent their entire lives inside, deprived of natural habitats and foods.

For centuries, cows lived outside in small groups, eating grass. Today, kept in larger groups, they are invariably inside and fed a grain and soya-based diet. The problem of feeding this unnatural diet to a cow is that it leads to inflammation of the wall of the rumen, impairs liver function and creates acidosis. Once this happens, the immune system is weakened, making the cows more susceptible to disease. Health problems caused by a grain diet can be managed by drugs, but of course a much better solution would be to feed cows their natural diet.

Industrial farms producing meat, dairy and eggs come at a high cost to both animals and to us. Our lack of understanding of the pain we directly or indirectly cause animals reflects a deeper spiritual disorder in our collective psyche. If we remove the respect for life from agriculture, we also remove its soul.

Many farmers grow a single crop in a field at a time. This is known as monocropping; the benefits to the farmers are a reduction in costs and an increase in profit. Monocropping can involve rotation, where monocultures of various crops are rotated around on a field each year, or else the same type of crop is grown in the same place year after year. Continuous monocropping exhausts nutrients from the earth and leaves soil weak and unable to support healthy plant growth. Because soil structure and quality is so poor, farmers turn to chemical fertilisers to encourage plant growth.

Monocropping has led to a decrease in diversity of crops. The last hundred years have seen the disappearance of 75% of the world's crop varieties, and just four crops combined – wheat, rice, barley and maize – cover almost 40% of all crop land. Three of these – wheat, rice and maize – account for 60% of the calories we consume. Plant biodiversity increases productivity in a wide range of growing conditions, which is absolutely essential in the face of climate change to grow enough food.

We are all aware of the fragile position that exists on planet Earth, be it conscious or unconscious. Our awareness over the last few years has become an increasingly stronger movement for change. More and more people are remembering a different relationship with the land and reclaiming the spiritual roots of agriculture, bringing back purpose and meaning to the growing of food.

Organic farming

At the heart of an organic farm is a healthy, fertile soil. This is achieved through rotation of crops, growth of a mixture of different crops and the addition of organic matter such as manure or compost. In addition, rather than leaving the soil bare, which allows nutrients to be washed away, green manure crops are grown. Green manure crops like clover are particularly good at fixing nitrogen from the atmosphere. These methods of developing nutrient-rich soils create strong, healthy crops, free from disease and pests, so no application of chemicals is needed. In any case, the use of pesticides is banned under organic regulations. Organic farms have a high standard of animal welfare; the routine use of drugs, antibiotics and wormers is banned. Preventative methods are used instead, including moving animals to fresh pasture and keeping smaller herd and flock sizes. Biodiversity is encouraged on an organic farm and genetically modified crops and ingredients in feed are banned.

There has been a long-standing argument that organic farming produces lower yields. There are a myriad of studies from around the world showing that organic farms can produce about as much, and in some cases much more, than farms that use chemicals. There are often lower yields in the first few years of converting to organic farming, but this is because the soil and biodiversity take time to recover.

Strict regulations, known as 'standards', define what organic farmers can and cannot do – and they place a strong emphasis on the protection of wildlife and the environment. The area of land is certified as organic worldwide is just 9%; in the UK, just under 4% of land is farmed organically with, at the last count, 3,740 organic farms. Other European countries have a greater proportion of organic farming; Austria has 18.5% organic land. There are many farmers that use organic principles but are not certified; this is especially true of farmers who only sell to local markets.

For foods to be labelled as organic, at least 95% of the ingredients must come from organically produced plants and organically reared animals.

The benefits of organic farming include reduced fossil fuel usage, increased biodiversity, weather resilience, no chemicals or toxic residues, increased nutrients, especially phytonutrients, and, of course, the food tastes better.

Permaculture

Permaculture is a consciously designed landscape that mimics the patterns and relationships found in nature. The ultimate purpose of permaculture is to develop a site until it meets all the needs of its inhabitants, including food, shelter and fuel. It is rooted in an ethic of caring for people, caring for planet Earth and investing surplus back into systems.

Permaculture is more often practised in indigenous villages, on smallholdings, on urban farms and in community gardens, and this is primarily for sustenance. There are larger farms that use permaculture as a guiding principle, though, in general, commercial-scale permaculture is not common.

Multi-layered forest gardens are a form of permaculture. The garden floor is covered with low growing fruits, such as strawberries, and vegetables; above them, there is a shrub layer. A bit higher up are the fruit trees, such as apples, pears, medlars and quinces. Finally there is the canopy of trees that aren't producing food but recycle nutrients through their root system and leaf litter.

Natural farming

Natural farming is based on the philosophy of Masanobu Fukuoka, who, through careful observation and experimentation, developed simple, effective techniques that produced abundant and healthy crops without the use of pesticides, chemical fertilisers, prepared compost, weeding or tilling. Fukuoka's seminal work, *The One Straw Revolution*, has influenced readers worldwide for 40 years with its deeply spiritual and practical accounting of natural farming.

Natural farming and permaculture have a lot of similarities despite very different approaches. Permaculture relies on the human intellect to create a strategy for living abundantly and sustainably within nature. Fukuoka saw the human intellect as the main culprit in separating humanity from nature and preferred to keep human decision-making out of the process.

Fukuoka believed that natural farming proceeded from the spiritual health of the individual. He considered the healing of the land and the journey of the human spirit to be one process: 'Natural farming is not just for growing crops,' he said. 'It is for the cultivation and perfection of human beings.' Natural systems have had millions of years to evolve; nature invites us to watch, listen, and learn.

Shumei Natural Agriculture

Natural Agriculture, which founder Mokichi Okada called 'the art of agriculture,' is the practice of building a balanced partnership with the soil, plants and other living things on and around a farm.

There are three pillars that support Natural Agriculture. The first is to practise and receive the spiritual healing jyorei, the second is to put yourself in the presence of beauty through artistic pursuit, and the third is to practise and eat foods of Natural Agriculture.

The first lesson of Natural Agriculture is that nature already has all it needs to survive; no chemicals, hybrid seeds, manure or other additives are needed, as plants and soils have a natural ability to heal and sustain themselves. The work of the Natural Agriculture farmer is to optimise these abilities, for example, saving and replanting seed so that a plant is able to adapt to its environment over successive seasons.

While Natural Agriculture may use natural compost such as leaves and grasses, it does not use manure because it does not believe this benefits the natural soil. Materials like leaves and stalks from vegetable matter are used not as a nutrient but to keep the soil moist, warm and soft. The principal belief is that everything needed by the plant for growth is already present in the soil, fully formed or with potential. Each year, through the practice of Natural Agriculture, the condition of the soil improves without extra feeding. Okado's Natural Agriculture is similar to Fukuoka's natural farming, the main difference being that Okado adds no nutrients to the soil whereas Fukuoka promotes the use of green manure crops like clover and alfalfa.

Natural Agriculture works at understanding the subtle relationships that exist among all the elements involved in growing food: the earth, sun, rain, wind, the farmer, the people who eat the food and the society in which they live. Its purpose is to foster the health and well-being of all these elements.

Biodynamic agriculture

Developed by Rudolph Steiner, biodynamic agriculture is a spiritual and ecological approach that treats the farm as an organism. This holistic system is founded on a closed loop, where no inputs are brought on to the farm. Soil fertility is built through cover crops and on farm animal manure. The biodynamic movement is practised worldwide in gardens, vineyards and farms of all kinds in a wide variety of different environments.

Preparations made from fermented manure, minerals and herbs are used to help restore and harmonise the vital life forces of the farm and to enhance the nutrition, quality and flavour of the food being raised. Biodynamic farmers follow the rhythms of nature and recognise the subtle influences of the wider cosmos on soil, plant and animal health. They use nine homoeopathic preparations to treat compost, soil and plants, and they think in terms of processes and forces, as opposed to substances.

Biodynamics is not just a holistic agricultural system but also a potent movement for new thinking and practices in all aspects of life connected to food and agriculture. Community-supported agriculture (CSA), for example, was pioneered by biodynamic farmers. CSA is a model of food production and distribution in which members and farmers work together on behalf of the Earth and each other. The farmer grows the food and the members share the harvest. Woven into the CSA model is the notion of shared risk: in most CSAs, members pay up front for a year's harvest and the farmers do their best to provide an abundant box of produce each week. The idea of shared risk is part of what creates a sense of community among members and between members and the farmers.

Biodynamics has an independent certification system managed worldwide by Demeter International. The Demeter certification program was established in 1928, and so was the first ecological label for organically produced foods. Biodynamic agriculture differs from organic agriculture in its spiritual, mystical, and astrological orientation.

The healthiest food systems foster sustainable relationships among plants, animals, farmers and everyone who cooks and eats. We have distanced ourselves from growing food and have lost sight of the multiple layers of relationships that are involved in bringing food to the table. Growing and eating food in appreciation of the myriad of connections that are involved enlivens our relationship to food, it becomes more life-enriching and we move closer to an ecological way of living – a regenerative way of life that is rooted in our relationship to all life on Earth.

Ways you can help support healthier growing systems

- Eat organic or biodynamically grown food
- Grow fruit and vegetables in your garden
- Support local farmers' markets
- Join a CSA and enjoy a weekly collection of fresh produce
- Find an allotment and grow your own fruit and vegetables
- Join a community garden or urban farm
- Volunteer to help with school gardens
- Learn loads about organic farming by volunteering on an organic farm

later years

As you grow older, your body becomes less forgiving, so eating to meet your nutritional needs at this time of life is really important to ensure good health. Generally, as you age, less energy is needed and appetites are smaller, so eating nutrient-dense food is vital to help ensure an easy and enjoyable time in later years.

Colourful vegetables and fruits

The unstable compounds free radicals can cause a great deal of damage to our cells. Free radicals are produced in our bodies through normal cellular metabolism. In addition, the body can accumulate free radicals from environmental sources, including industrial waste, car exhausts and cigarette smoke. Antioxidants neutralise free radicals, and without enough of these vitally important molecules, cells begin to behave abnormally, the body becomes damaged and degenerative disease manifests. So it is important to make sure the diet contains plenty of potent antioxidants, which come from eating a wide variety of colourful vegetables and fruits. Selenium is a particularly important antioxidant, and deficiency can be a problem as crops grown in selenium-deficient soils will themselves be deficient. Selenium is found in mushrooms, beans, asparagus and whole grains.

Homocysteine

The amino acid homocysteine is made in the body from the amino acid methionine. Eggs, cheese, fish, sunflower seeds, yoghurt and meat are all rich sources of methionine. Homocysteine is then converted in the blood to S-Adenosyl methionine (SAMe) and glutathione. SAMe helps prevent depression, liver damage and arthritis, and glutathione is a powerful antioxidant. Conversion requires adequate supplies of zinc, folate, Vitamin B2 and Vitamin B12. Poor conversion can result in elevated levels of homocysteine, which is a risk factor for heart attack, stroke, diabetes, neurological conditions and depression.

Elderly people are often deficient in Vitamin B12. Low stomach acid or bacterial imbalance in the large intestine can cause Vitamin B12 malabsorption. If you suspect you have B12 deficiency, the first step is to get tested. If you are B12 deficient, the next step is to identify the mechanism causing the deficiency, then work out the appropriate form of treatment, either by supplementation (injection, oral, sublingual – a tablet under the tongue – or nasal) or increasing food sources of Vitamin B12, which are primarily foods of animal origin.

Sugar

Sugar plays havoc with blood glucose, resulting in a constantly elevated blood glucose level, which predisposes the body to degenerative disease. In addition, sugar is a proinflammatory, creating inflammation by forming advanced glycation end products known as AGEs.

AGEs are complex compounds formed when a protein reacts with sugar. The body tries to break down AGEs, and in the process immune cells secrete large amounts of inflammatory chemicals. It is actually this process that is often the cause of ageing. AGEs can occur anywhere in the body, resulting in varied conditions including arthritis, cataracts, memory loss or wrinkled skin.

Gut function

The composition of your gut flora changes as you grow older. Often, the levels of friendly bacteria diminish, leading to a gradual decrease in the absorption of nutrients through the intestinal wall. Fermented foods, however, can help counteract these problems, yoghurt, kefir and fermented vegetables all being good choices. Fermented foods also supply enzymes, which can help counteract the deterioration of digestive enzyme production as you grow older. Slower bowel movements caused by lack of liquid and dietary fibre, together with a more sedentary lifestyle, can often lead to constipation. Pulses, vegetables (especially cabbage, collards and broccoli) along with fruits (in particular raspberries and pears) are all an excellent source of dietary fibre. Drinking plenty of water each day with the addition of herb teas and enjoying a daily walk will help to support gut function and prevent constipation.

Osteoporosis

To prevent osteoporosis, our bones need to be given the right nutrition. Brittle bones caused by osteoporosis can lead to breakages and a greatly impaired life. To help maintain bone health as you grow older, calcium is of special importance. It is found in sardines, yoghurt, dark green leafy vegetables and sea vegetables, especially wakame. Vitamin D is equally important and found in eggs, oily fish, shiitake mushrooms and daily sun exposure. In addition, bone health requires Vitamin K2, found in green leafy vegetables; zinc, found in eggs, pumpkin seeds and whole grains; phosphorous, found in oats, seafood and nuts; and magnesium, found in whole grains and dark green leafy vegetables.

Joint mobility

Osteoarthritis can be debilitating and lead to a significant decrease in the quality of life. Statistics suggest that over a third of adults, and as many as 85% of people over 80 years of age, suffer to some degree from osteoarthritis. Omega-3 fatty acids are essential to support joint mobility; they are found in fatty fish, which is why it is often recommended to eat fish such as salmon, mackerel, herring, sardines and fresh tuna on a regular basis. If you choose not to eat fatty fish, make sure you eat a diet rich in flax, hemp and dark green leafy vegetables.

Brain and cognitive function

The brain loses volume as neurons die and this is inevitable; however, there isn't necessarily a loss of cognitive ability, and many people retain full brain-based skills until they are very old. An ageing brain can, however, result in a myriad of problems, including decreased mental ability, confusion and dementia, all of which can cause a major impact on the quality of life in later years.

Help support the brain and cognitive function by ensuring an adequate intake of omega-3 fatty acids and protein (fatty fish or hemp are a good source of both), and ensure that your diet includes foods full of minerals and vitamins. Particularly important are the B vitamins, especially B12, folate and Vitamin D.

Heart health

The older you are, the greater your risk of suffering a heart attack, but there is plenty of evidence to show that the food you choose to eat can make a big difference to heart health. A healthy heart diet should include plenty of omega-3 fatty acids; eating oily fish on a regular basis has repeatedly shown to be beneficial, but, if you do not eat fish, include plenty of hemp and flax in your diet. Vitamin D is especially important, along with bright-coloured vegetables and dark green leafy vegetables.

In studies of cultures such as the Hunzakuts in Pakistan or the Okinawa in Japan, researchers have found that people can live active lives for more than a hundred years. Simple, unrefined diets, exercise, fresh air and pure water are contributory factors, but so too is living with a deep sense of spirituality, meaning and purpose.

In indigenous cultures, elders have experiences of rituals and rites, an understanding of nature's rhythms and a deep connection to place. This valuable knowledge is passed on to the young, enabling cultures to remain intact and integrating elders into the community. In Western culture our disconnection from the land means this knowledge base has shifted. The latter years are an invaluable stage in life as they harbour a myriad of stories to be shared, giving an opportunity for us all to come together and shape a future that sustains everyone.

People are aged by the culture they live in. A greater sense of well-being, fulfilment and general health comes from being part of a community that fosters respect, values the breadth of human diversity and creates a caring, supportive and loving culture in which elders can live.

nourishing meals in a bowl

Each recipe makes 2 bowls

SPRING

Baked eggs with spinach Ⓔ Ⓓ

800g spinach
40g butter
handful of chervil
grating of nutmeg
2 large eggs
2 tablespoons yoghurt
50g feta
salt and pepper

Preheat the oven to 180°C/350°F/Gas mark 6.

Roughly chop the spinach. Melt the butter in a pan, add half the spinach and allow to wilt before adding the remainder and wilting. Strain the spinach and reserve the liquid. Return the liquid to the pan and reduce until just a teaspoon is left, then swirl in the butter, toss in the spinach, add the chervil and season with the nutmeg, salt and pepper.

Divide the mixture between 2 ovenproof bowls. Make a hollow in the spinach mixture in each bowl and crack an egg into each one. Put a tablespoon of yoghurt on each one and top with the feta cheese.

Bake for 10–15 minutes or until the eggs are cooked to your liking.

SUMMER

Quinoa tabbouleh

170g quinoa
4 large tomatoes, seeded and diced
4 spring onions, finely shredded
half a cucumber, finely diced
1 large bunch of flat-leaf parsley, chopped
12 mint leaves, finely shredded
juice and zest of 1 lemon
salt and pepper

Cook the quinoa in plenty of water for about 15 minutes or until just cooked; drain well and put into a bowl.

Add the tomatoes, spring onions, cucumber, parsley, mint and lemon, mix well, season and leave for 30 minutes. Divide between 2 bowls and top with the hemp seeds.

AUTUMN

Kale with sweet potatoes and hazelnuts ⓝ

2 medium sweet potatoes
1 tablespoon olive oil
250g kale (cavolo nero is particularly good)
2 handfuls of sprouted alfalfa
3 tablespoons hazelnuts, very lightly toasted
    and roughly chopped
salt and pepper

For the dressing
4 tablespoons olive oil
1 tablespoon balsamic vinegar
1 teaspoon Dijon mustard
1 teaspoon honey
2 cloves garlic, very finely chopped
a good pinch of salt and ¼ teaspoon
    black pepper

Preheat the oven to 200°C/400°F/Gas mark 6.

Toss the sweet potatoes with the oil and spread on a baking tray. Roast for 20 minutes, remove from oven, gently stir, and return to oven until soft in the middle and crisp on the edges.

Discard any large stalks from the kale. Bring a deep saucepan of water to a rolling boil and blanch the kale for a minute. Drain, refresh in cold water, shred finely and place in a bowl.

Put the dressing ingredients in a jar with a lid and shake well to mix. Pour it over the kale and gently mix. Divide the kale between 2 bowls, pile the sweet potato and then the alfalfa on top, and sprinkle over the hazelnuts.

White bean soup

1 onion, peeled and chopped
2 cloves garlic, finely chopped
3 tablespoons olive oil
½ teaspoon thyme leaves
2 leeks, cleaned and cut into fine rings
2 celery stalks, chopped
2 carrots, chopped
175g dried white beans, soaked overnight (use
     cannellini or butter beans)
1 litre vegetable stock
1 bay leaf
2 strips wakame
5 sage leaves
handful of parsley, chopped
chilli powder

Cook the onion and garlic in the oil until soft. Add the thyme, the remaining vegetables, and the well-drained beans, and stir well. Pour over the stock, add the bay leaf and wakame and bring to the boil. Simmer gently for 1 hour or until the beans are soft.

Cool for 10 minutes, remove the wakame, then whizz the soup in a food processor until smooth. You may have to do this in 2 batches.

Return to the pan. Finely shred the cooked wakame, and add to the soup with the finely shredded sage and the chopped parsley. Gently reheat, season if necessary and serve in warmed bowls topped with a sprinkling of chilli powder.

Nutrient-dense foods

Nutrient density refers to the amount of essential nutrients for the given volume of food. Nutrient-dense foods have lots of nutrients and generally fewer calories. Energy-dense foods mostly have more calories for the volume of food, and generally fewer nutrients.

Energy needs decrease as one becomes more elderly, resulting in a smaller food intake. It is important to choose nutrient-dense foods, those with a high ratio of nutrients to energy, to ensure adequate nutrient intake.

Five nutrient-dense foods:

Kale	Kale is one of the most nutrient-dense vegetables you can eat, with large amounts of vitamins, minerals and cancer-fighting compounds.
Sea vegetables	Vegetables from the sea are highly nutritious – they are particularly high in iodine, which is essential for optimal thyroid function. Wakame is a very good source of calcium.
Whole eggs	Whole eggs are loaded with vitamins, minerals and various powerful nutrients. They are a good source of choline, an important brain nutrient. They also contain high-quality protein.
Quinoa	Quinoa is rich in protein, essential fatty acids, iron, magnesium and manganese. Quinoa contains the amino acid lysine, which is often lacking in grains and is gluten free.
Sprouts	Sprouts are one of the most nutrient-dense foods you can eat.

sea vegetables

Earth, the magnificent blue planet, has 70% of its surface covered by oceans. It was in these waters over several million years ago that the first plants on earth, called blue-green algae, developed. Over time they evolved to carry out photosynthesis, bringing oxygen to our planet.

Sea vegetables, sometimes known as seaweed or algae, are plants with a simple structure that grow and feed in water. These plants have been eaten by coastal people since prehistoric times. Today, over a hundred species of red, brown and green seaweed are used worldwide as food, especially in Japan, Korea, Norway, Scotland, Ireland, Iceland, China and New Zealand. Traditional seaweed dishes are also found in California, Maine, Nova Scotia, Brittany and Wales.

The sea is the richest repository of the earth's minerals, and sea vegetables are the richest source of organic mineral salts in nature. All sea vegetables are an excellent source of calcium and iodine, but many other minerals are found in high levels including iron, phosphorus, potassium, manganese, zinc, boron and silicon. Sea vegetables are also an excellent source of vitamins, polyunsaturated fatty acids, enzymes and chlorophyll.

Over one-fifth of the global population is living on iodine-deficient soils and, according to the WHO, 72% of the global population is iodine-deficient. The thyroid, along with many other glands and tissues in the body, needs iodine; it is found and used in every hormonal receptor in the body. Iodine helps destroy harmful bacteria; a lack of iodine can be a contributory factor in fatigue, colds and infections. Iodine is an important nutrient for the brain, and mental sluggishness can be a symptom of deficiency. Recent collaborative research between the Universities of Surrey and Bristol found that mild to moderate iodine deficiency appears sufficient to affect foetal brain development and concluded that iodine was an important nutrient for women of childbearing age. Regular consumption of sea vegetables is a good way of increasing iodine levels, though there are a small number of people, specifically those with selenium deficiency, for whom eating iodine-rich seaweed could be a problem.

Plant substances known as lignans are found in sea vegetables. In the body, they block the chemical oestrogen that can lead to breast cancer. The research of Dr Jane Teas from Harvard University suggests that kelp consumption might be a factor in the lower rates of breast cancer in Japan.

Alginic acid, found in sea vegetables, helps detoxification in the body. A study from McGill University in Canada shows that sea vegetables are good at helping the body eliminate the radioactive chemical strontium. The alginic acid binds with heavy metals like cadmium and lead, found predominantly in the environment.

Alginates derived from seaweeds are used extensively in the food processing industry for their water holding, gelling, emulsifying and stabilising properties. They are used to stabilise ice cream, improve the head on beer, allow fast setting in puddings and emulsify oils. In the list of ingredients, their E-numbers are 400 to 405. Alginates are also used in the cosmetic, medical, paint and other industries.

Foraging for seaweed is fun and it is very satisfying to harvest such a nutritious bounty. If you do, make sure you forage in clean, safe waters, otherwise source from companies that test to ensure all products reach international safety levels.

Dulse

Beautiful, soft waves of purple dulse grow attached to rocks in the North Atlantic – it is a very easy sea vegetable to add to your diet; it doesn't need soaking, and it has a sweet and tender flavour. It has been harvested as a medicine and food for thousands of years, used traditionally in Ireland, Iceland and parts of Canada. It is harvested and generally dried, but it can also be eaten straight off the rocks.

If you harvest your own dulse, make sure you collect it from a clean seashore and always gently cut away from the rock, leaving a little bit of the stalk so that the dulse can continue to grow. Alternatively, it is easy to source packets of dried dulse.

Kombu

Kombu is part of the kelp family, which consists of over 800 species. It can be used in salads or added to soups and stews. It has a mild spicy-salty flavour and it can be used as a replacement for salt. When you cook beans, add a sheet of kombu to the pot; it is the glutamic acid in kombu that helps to make the beans more digestible and less gassy.

Glutamate may sound similar to monosodium glutamate (MSG), but they are very different. Glutamate is a naturally occurring substance, whereas MSG is a chemically synthesised product.

Wakame

Wakame seaweed grows in abundance worldwide. It is particularly popular in Japan where it is a typical ingredient of miso soup. Wakame is generally bought dried and then reconstituted by soaking in water or by simply adding to stocks, soups and stews.

Wakame, like all seaweeds, is a rich source of minerals and vitamins. It is a particularly good source of calcium and contains a good balance of magnesium to enable proper absorption of calcium, thus helping to build strong bones.

For people who prefer not to eat foods of animal origin, it makes a good addition to the diet, providing a good source of protein and the essential fatty acid omega-3. The pigment fucoxanthin, found in wakame, improves insulin resistance and is thought to be helpful in losing weight.

Nori

This is the species the Japanese use to form the wrapping for sushi. The Welsh call it laver and traditionally turn it into a sort of porridge, mixing it with oatmeal and frying it in bacon fat for breakfast.

Cultivated nori is big business in Japan, but it is also cultivated in the United States. Nori is readily available, dried in paper-thin sheets. For the best results you should toast the sheets before use, though you can purchase ready-toasted nori sheets.

Among the marine flora, nori is one of the richest in protein and also contains the powerful antioxidant Vitamin C and the compound taurine, which is found in bile. Bile is essential for fat digestion as well as the absorption of fat-soluble vitamins.

Irish moss

Irish moss, or carrageen, is found along the rocky parts of the Atlantic coasts of Europe and North America. The colour varies from a dark purplish red to brown, green, yellow or white depending on the exposure to sunlight. Irish moss is widely used in all sorts of food products because it has emulsifying and gelling properties.

Irish moss has many healing benefits: it is a soothing aid to all mucous membranes and is said to ease nausea, indigestion and constipation. In Ireland it is traditionally used as a cold and cough remedy.

Sea lettuce

Sea lettuce is found worldwide and is a bright green, cellophane-like leaf similar to land lettuce. This delicate green seaweed is used predominately in the Far East, Chile and the West Indies, cooked in soups and eaten raw in salads. In parts of China it is used as a medicine against fevers.

Sea lettuce is high in minerals, vitamins and protein, but as it likes to grow in nutrient-rich water including polluted areas, make sure you know where any sea lettuce you eat has been harvested.

Marsh samphire

Marsh samphire is native to North America, South Africa, South Asia and Europe. It grows around the coast of Britain in marshes, and the bright green, skinny succulent plant is best eaten young. It is not really a seaweed, but it does grow in tidal zones, often around estuaries. It is delicious raw, but it is often briefly cooked, then tossed in butter or oil before eating.

water – the gift of life

Water, a mysterious crystalline living organism that nurtures all life, is the lifeblood of Mother Earth. Water is everywhere; it is in the atmosphere as humidity, clouds and rain, it forms rivers, seas, glaciers and icecaps, and it is in the soil, plants, trees and animals. Our bodies are two-thirds water, but in terms of molecules, we're more than 99% water molecules.

Water defies the law of physics, which dictates that the solid phase of a substance will be denser than its liquid state and that something solid will sink in liquid – not so with water. Like all other liquids, it shrinks as it cools, but when it reaches 4°C (39°F), water reaches its maximum density. Beyond this point its density begins to diminish instead of increase. As water freezes, the oxygen and hydrogen atoms re-form to create a lighter structure so that ice floats; this action of freezing from the top down on lakes and ponds allows fish and life to continue to flourish under the water. It takes a great amount of energy to turn ice into liquid and to bring water to the boil. The temperature at which the greatest amount of heat or cold is required to change water's temperature is 37°C (99°F), which is why our blood, which is 90% water, survives when exposed to extreme temperatures.

Ancient civilizations honoured water and worshipped this life-giving substance which was integral to their rites and rituals. They shared their respect for water through myths and stories passed down from generation to generation. These people held the magical transforming substance of water sacred. Today, water is still significant to many religions, but in general we are less respectful of water's life-giving force.

Planet Earth is part of the cosmos and, as such, is constantly communicating with everything that happens in our solar system. The cyclic phases of the moon and planetary constellations have a very clearly defined effect on planet Earth. Theodor Schwenk, a scientific and spiritual explorer, demonstrated that water is the sense organ of the planet and developed methods which clearly showed variations in water response to changes in planetary constellation.

The strong cyclical pattern of water on Earth creates a continuous movement of water on, above and below the surface of the Earth. Water evaporates from the seas up into the atmosphere

where it condenses, forming clouds and rain. The rain falls to the ground; some flows back into the seas via river systems, whilst some permeates into the ground and replenishes the groundwater reserves before eventually returning to the surface and feeding back into the river systems. This cycle is now being interrupted; water is running off the land without permeating through the ground, resulting in floods and water shortages. In Europe and elsewhere, the single biggest cause of floods and water shortage is the way we manage our landscapes.

In many areas, intensive chemical farming and land drainage have destroyed the soil's ability to capture and store rainwater. In addition, trees have been cut down, curtailing the percolation of water through the ground. Man-made disasters can be prevented through ecological land management, which can halt and reverse the position we find ourselves in through not working in harmony with nature. In Europe, the European Water Framework Directive has been set up to hopefully halt the lowering of the water table, stop floods and protect against soil erosion.

Natural water tumbles and falls through vortexes of energy and magnetic fields on Earth and is exposed to energy from the sun. During this process, nature adds minerals and oxygen to the water. The result is a highly structured water, mineralised and oxygenated and full of energy and vitality. Health-giving water is attuned to the cosmos and energetically charged, but our modern water treatments that use chemicals and our transport systems of straight pressurised pipes do not allow this to happen.

How do we ensure we drink high-quality, health-promoting water?

Tap water is unlikely to have the purity essential for health, as it is treated with a large number of chemicals in order to kill bacteria and other microorganisms. Chlorine affects the metabolism of fat and hormonal activity; it inhibits the actions of certain enzymes and can affect the bacteria in the gut. In addition, water has the potential to contain contaminants, including hormones and pesticides, and nitrates that leach into water as residues from artificial fertilisers. A certain degree of purity can be achieved by using filters or purifiers.

A filter is a substance like carbon or charcoal which removes certain types of chemicals and toxins from water. Different types of carbon and carbon filters remove different contaminants, but no one type removes them all. Carbon filters do not remove viruses or bacteria, but an ultraviolet water filter will. A purifier removes a minimum of 90–95% of all contaminants in water. Purifying

technologies include reverse osmosis and distillation. Reverse osmosis is the process of filtering water under pressure through a semipermeable membrane, allowing water to pass through but rejecting bacteria and other contaminants. Distillation involves boiling the water and then condensing the steam into a clean container. Distilled water is not very energy efficient, and a major problem is that it removes important minerals. If you use this method, it is worth adding a few drops of a sea mineral liquid to your water. These various treatments will go a long way to remove impurities, but they will not create a living water that truly nourishes health.

It is through the spiralling movement that water maintains its energy as living water. Rudolf Steiner introduced the vortex principle to farmers in the 1920s for use in biodynamic agricultural preparations. Stirring water with a wooden handle in a large glass or ceramic container, first in one direction to form a vortex and then reversing direction until another deep vortex forms in the opposite direction, the energy of the vortex is absorbed into the water, creating a vibrant, living water.

Rudolf Steiner also suggested the use of a flow form to simulate the action of mountain streams and re-energise water. George Adams and then John Wilkes evolved the flow form, which sends water cascading from a reservoir through several levels of spiral formations (preferably whilst exposed to the sun) to create an energised water. Andreas Schulz has shown through crystal analysis, a method of testing quality capable of withstanding judgement by scientific criteria, how the spiralling movement improves the structure and quality of water.

It is possible to energise the water in your home. The double egg vortexer is two egg-shaped glasses linked together. With the bottom egg cradled in the palm of one hand, a small rotation movement on the top egg with your other hand creates a vortex and moves the water from the top to the bottom egg. This is repeated alternately clockwise and anticlockwise, and the positive and negative charges created bring energy back into the water. You can also buy water vortex jugs.

The research work of Jacques Benveniste and Dr David Schweitzer has proven that water acts as a liquid memory system capable of storing information. Because water molecules have a positive and negative pole, they behave like tiny magnets. Molecules attach to neighbouring molecules and form clusters of several hundred molecules. These clusters are very sensitive to vibrational

influences and give water the ability to store information.

This helps us understand homoeopathy. In homoeopathy a substance is diluted time after time until eventually there is no molecule of the original substance left. Countless experiments have shown, however, that it still has an effect. Flower essences are vibrational remedies where water is imprinted with the 'signature' of a specific flower and used to treat a variety of emotional disorders and temperaments. Flower essences affect the physical body via the emotions, while homoeopathic remedies resonate more with the molecular structure of the cellular body.

Water can carry harmful information as well. Dr Wolfgang Ludwig in Germany has shown that not only do the physical pollutants in water have a damaging effect on our health, but so does the water which has been exposed to those pollutants because the cluster structure has taken on those vibrational imprints.

Re-energising and revitalising water through the action of a vortex retunes the molecular cluster structure of water and erases detrimental information patterns. A simple way to help re-energise water is to place a quartz crystal in a jug of water for 8–12 hours. You can additionally infuse the water by leaving the jug in sunlight or moonlight. Schulz has shown through crystal analysis that quartz produces a positive change in water quality.

Bottled water

There are different classifications of bottled water. Natural mineral water comes from underground sources and is free of harmful bacteria. There is no minimum level for the water's mineral contents. Some filtering is permitted, and the water may be carbonated to make it sparkling, but it cannot be disinfected. Spring water simply has to conform to the same quality standards as tap water and can come from any source from natural springs through to mains water. Naturally carbonated natural mineral water may be treated, but the original gas is reincorporated into the water afterwards, whereas carbonated natural mineral water is a natural mineral water made effervescent by the addition of carbon dioxide from another source.

Britain consumes 3 billion litres of bottled water per year, typically retailing at 500 times more than the price of tap water. In the UK, the market for bottled water is £2 billion, which of course earns huge yearly profits for big brands. The cost to the environment is enormous; endless water bottle production depends on oil and this, together with transportation, causes an estimated release of 350,000 tonnes of carbon dioxide into the atmosphere per year. Bottled water is just not a sustainable product. Neither is it necessarily, as is often assumed, a healthy alternative to tap water. Bottled water may be a good source of particular minerals, however, just like mains water, being trapped in a container means there is no life force. If the water is bottled in plastic, the water will assimilate some of the signature of the packaging; in addition, some unhealthy chemicals can leach from plastic into the water.

at-a-glance vitamins and minerals

Vitamin A as Beta-carotene	eye and skin health; antioxidant *Three good sources:* carrots, watercress, squash
Vitamin B1, Thiamine	aids protein metabolism; essential for energy, brain function and digestion *Three good sources:* beans, cauliflower, peas
Vitamin B2, Riboflavin	energy production; healthy skin, hair, nails and eyes *Three good sources:* peas, watercress, cabbage
Vitamin B3, Niacin	energy production; digestive health *Three good sources:* sprouted wheat, asparagus, tomatoes
Vitamin B5, Pantothenic acid	energy production – fat metabolism maintains nervous system *Three good sources:* eggs, avocado, broccoli
Vitamin B6	protein metabolism; hormone production *Three good sources:* cauliflower, spinach, peppers
Vitamin B12	red blood cell formation; DNA synthesis *Three good sources:* yoghurt, cottage cheese, eggs
Folate	brain and nerve function; red blood cell formation *Three good sources:* whole wheat, broccoli, cauliflower
Vitamin C	boosts immune function; wound healing *Three good sources:* rosehips, cabbage, strawberries
Vitamin D	bone health *Three good sources:* shiitake, eggs, sunlight
Vitamin E	immune function; improves wound healing and fertility *Three good sources:* sunflower seeds, hemp seeds, almonds
Vitamin K	controls blood clotting *Three good sources:* broccoli, Brussels sprouts, cauliflower
Biotin	healthy skin, hair and nerves; helps make efficient use of sugar *Three good sources:* chard, eggs, sweetcorn
Calcium	strengthens bones; maintains acid-alkaline balance *Three good sources:* almonds, broccoli, sesame

Chromium	essential in regulating blood sugar by helping insulin transport glucose into the cells *Three good sources:* whole grains, potatoes, broccoli
Copper	regulates blood pressure and heart rate; relieves aching muscles; reduces cramps *Three good sources:* whole grains, peas, tomatoes
Iron	essential for the blood and energy *Three good sources:* dried apricots, cocoa powder, almonds
Magnesium	important in muscle and nerve activity; strengthens bones and teeth *Three good sources:* whole wheat products, almonds, green leafy vegetables
Manganese	forms healthy bones, cartilage, tissues and nerves; important for insulin production *Three good sources:* blackberries, nuts, pulses
Phosphorous	forms healthy bones; builds muscle tissue, aids metabolism *Three good sources:* nuts, eggs, whole wheat products
Potassium	maintains water balance; involved in metabolism, proper functioning of the heart and elimination *Three good sources:* dried fruits, raw vegetables, molasses
Selenium	antioxidant; stimulates the immune system to fight infection *Three good sources:* eggs, molasses, sunflower seeds
Sodium	maintains water balance; helps nerve functioning and muscle contraction *Three good sources:* miso, sea vegetables, celery
Zinc	important for healing component of many enzymes; maintains healthy liver *Three good sources:* pumpkin seeds, ginger root, raw chocolate
Molybdenum	assists uric acid excretion; reduces risk of dental caries *Three good sources:* buckwheat, beans, lentils
Sulphur	involved in the formation of bile acids; needed for fat digestion and absorption *Three good sources:* rocket, garlic, onions
Iodine	thyroid mineral and assists the immune system *Three good sources:* sea vegetables, asparagus, kale
Boron	assists with calcium assimilation *Three good sources:* cauliflower, raisins, almonds

seven flavours of winter

Beetroot

Deliciously sweet with earthy notes, crimson beetroot is a firm winter favourite. Crisp and juicy when raw, it works well in juices, smoothies and salads. Roasting brings out the natural sweetness and the dense flavour marries well with horseradish, apple, ginger, nuts, balsamic vinegar and creamy cheeses. Beetroot contains the mineral silica, which is important for musculo-skeletal health and reducing the risk of osteoporosis.

Kale

Kales of all sort, abundant in the winter months, are best eaten freshly harvested as the sparkling green flavour is soon lost and the flavour becomes flat and almost bitter. Available at other times of the year, it is, however, at its absolute best when a light frost has touched the leaves, making them sweeter. Kale has a very high nutritional value with a good supply of calcium, folic acid, and Vitamins A and C.

Onion

This wonderful bulb vegetable is one of the oldest edible food sources known to man. Onions are found in so many recipes and have been used in traditional medicines since ancient times for their health-promoting and curative properties. The sharp, pungent smell and taste of onions is due to the sulphur compound allyl propyl disulphide, which helps lower blood sugar (this is the compound that makes you cry!). Onions are high in chromium, an essential mineral that helps cells respond to glucose.

Quince

This is the fruit of winter. Too hard to eat raw, quince only works cooked; this gives you the opportunity to make comforting, cold weather puddings with them. Quince is not a big tree, rarely reaching a height of more than 12–15 feet, so you could grow one in a small garden. The fruits picked in the autumn will last well into the winter. The small, yellow, pear-shaped fruit is heavenly aromatic and, rather miraculously, when left to slowly cook, the flesh turns a glorious, deep crimson.

Sweet chestnut

Roasting chestnuts on a log fire on a frosty winter evening is very hard to beat. The sweet chestnut, which was introduced to the UK by the Romans, flourishes mostly in the warmer south. In contrast to other nuts and seeds, they are much lower in protein and fat; starchy, sweet and rich in flavour, chestnuts are nonetheless nourishing. They can be made into soups, added to grain dishes and used to make puddings, cakes, bread and porridge.

Celeriac

The knobbly, odd-shaped celeriac has a subtle, celery-like flavour with nutty overtones. Like parsnips, swede and potatoes, celeriac is a warming winter root vegetable. Try it as mash, in big-flavoured, slow-cooked dishes, or cut into matchsticks and tossed in a mustardy dressing. Celeriac contains Vitamins B1, B2 and E and is a very good source of fibre, magnesium, phosphorus, calcium and potassium.

Bay

These slightly bitter, strongly aromatic leaves are an essential winter flavouring for marinades, casseroles, soups, sauces, puddings and warming mulled drinks. Bay, parsley and thyme together make the classic bouquet garni. The bay tree has always had a reputation as a tree that protects against all evil. The Greeks and the Romans believed that the herb symbolises wisdom and peace – their heroes were crowned with wreathes of bay laurel, and the word 'laureate' derives from it.

sharing goodness

Sandra White

All winter I have been thinking about 'weeds'. Preparing to take on a new allotment for the first time, I have wondered how far I will go to ensure that my plot is a place where everything will have its full life for as long as possible, not simply the vegetables I want to grow. Aware that this goes against contemporary growing conventions, I have also wondered how far I will be allowed to go by neighbours and the site committee.

Since childhood, I have been told that everything growing in the soil feeds on, and so depletes, the vital elements within it – hence the various methods to replenish them through chemical or organic fertilisers. So it has made sense to reduce the competition for those nutrients while the vegetables grow, and all around me I see large patches of thick, black plastic sheets, covering the soil and ensuring that nothing else starts to grow before the vegetables can be started. I anticipate these sheets giving way to bare soil and know that my fellow growers will devote many hours to ensuring that all other plant-life does not flourish so that all the goodness in the soil will only be taken up by the vegetables they want to grow and eat.

Until relatively recently, my image of how plants grow in the soil has been quite simple – their roots spread down into the soil and drink up the nutrition to be found there. With better knowledge, this has been replaced by the kind of picture Daphne has painted for us of the millions of diverse microbes living in the soil, which themselves directly feed on the nutritious elements around them and convert these into a plant-soluble form so that the roots can then drink them in. Indeed, at the start of the season, the plants exude carbohydrates and sugars, which will attract suitable microbes to do that job for them, so a true symbiotic relationship exists at an unseen level in the soil without which nothing would grow. What makes sense to me now is that whichever plants – wild species, herbs and vegetables – thrive in a particular piece of soil will attract to themselves the microbe communities they need to enable this symbiotic relationship to prosper. The healthier the plants, the greater the microbe communities in terms of both strength and numbers.

The vital importance of biodiversity cannot be overstated. This is the very nature of life. Where there is uncultivated soil the world over, a myriad different plants grow together, intermingled, often intertwined. In a profound paradox, they at once support and compete with each other. Overall, aside from times of imbalance, they enhance each other on their evolutionary journeys and, through the cycles of their living and dying, along with the millions of other species on and among them, they comprise and enhance the soil. This is a virtuous circle in which vibrant, healthy soil grows vibrant, healthy plant life of all shapes and sizes; this provides vibrant, healthy food to other species, all of which transforms upon death into vibrant, healthy soil... One of the mysteries of the rainforests is that sometimes the depth of the soil is no more than a fine layer – and the immensity of life it supports bears testament to this circle.

In a sense, the almost religious practice of weeding vegetable patches equally bears testament to how little contemporary ecological understanding our society has taken in, for the implication of biodiversity is that vegetables will be enhanced by a community of plant life around them. Perhaps the Darwinian concept of 'survival of the fittest' and its emphasis on competition has taken hold so deeply that collectively we are unable to see the essential part that co-operation plays in life, evolution and health. I think that the almost unconscious story is that by ensuring that our vegetables 'win' by 'taking out' the competition, we strengthen our own chances of being 'winners' when we eat the fruit of our labours – the weeding that is relentless, back-breaking work!

What will it take to shift this mindset and its consequent practices? One element, I think, is to address our collective stories about larger nature and their emphasis on its 'red in tooth and claw'-ness in the animal, bird and insect kingdoms. We need to paint more pictures of symbiosis, which creates not only mutual dependence but also mutual improvement, as well as of the intrinsic character of the plant kingdom as abundant and trustworthy in specific ways. These qualities arise out of that essential paradox of competition and co-operation. With better ecological understanding of these interplays, we may discover within ourselves feelings of respect, gratitude and love for the biosphere within which we live. Then we might even want to share the soil's goodness with the other species that normally inhabit it. This is what has happened for me, and as these feelings have grown, so has an intense desire to uphold life itself, to make this the organising principle of my life.

This gives me the task of discovering how to live happily within larger nature, entering consciously into that symbiotic relationship and discovering how I can devote my human properties, the gifts of life and evolution, to enhance the lives of what grows around me as I receive their benefits. Those benefits are not simply nutritional – they are sensual, heart-lifting, soul-nourishing. They bring me a greater sense of trust and strengthen the ease with which I can allow things to pass through me, reducing the impacts of fear, competitiveness and possessiveness.

So, on my tiny piece of land on the allotment, rather than imposing myself, I intend to insert myself gently into it. I will experiment with not clearing the soil of all existing plant-life, instead only taking out enough to create the space I need to start my seeds. I will find ways to express my deep desire for all around me to be equally content and well. And I will explore how to drink in the beauty and sheer vibrancy of the manifold gifts of life, for which I want to say 'thank you'.

As an ecopsychologist, Sandra White's deep interest is in cultural change towards greater respect for and relationship with larger nature, so that upholding all life becomes a foundation for modern civilisation.

winter recipes

Apple, beetroot and ginger juice
Prune, spirulina and almond smoothie Ⓝ
Pear, kale and echinacea smoothie
Buckwheat flakes with almond milk Ⓝ
Sea vegetable salad Ⓢ
Apple, celery and walnut salad with
    almond mayonnaise Ⓝ
Winter salad with flaxseed and chilli dressing
Six flavour soup Ⓢ
Potato and kimchi gratin
Barley pilaf with winter squash, kale and
    red onions Ⓖ Ⓓ
Roast broccoli with tahini dressing Ⓢ
Sourdough drop scones Ⓖ Ⓔ
A winter sourdough rye Ⓖ
Linseed crackers with hemp pâté
Chocolate hemp brownie with chocolate
    hemp sorbet Ⓓ Ⓔ Ⓝ
Mulled apple juice

Ⓖ – contains gluten
Ⓓ – contains dairy
Ⓢ – contains soya
Ⓔ – contains eggs
Ⓝ – contains nuts

Apple, beetroot and ginger juice

Serves 1
2 apples
1 beetroot
half a thumb-sized piece of ginger

Cut up the apples but do not core or peel. Scrub, peel if necessary and cut the beetroot into pieces. Put all the ingredients through a juicer and drink at once.

···

Prune, spirulina and almond smoothie Ⓝ

Serves 1
6 prunes, soaked
1 teaspoon spirulina
150ml almond milk (see page 255)

In a food blender or smoothie maker, whizz all the ingredients together, adding a little prune soak water if necessary, until smooth. Pour into a glass and drink.

···

Pear, kale and echinacea smoothie

Serves 1
2 handfuls of kale, hard stalks removed and
    roughly chopped
1 pear, chopped
1 cup celery juice
juice of half a lemon
half a thumb-sized piece of ginger, sliced
10 drops echinacea tincture

In a food blender or smoothie maker, whizz all the ingredients together until smooth. Pour into a glass and drink.

Buckwheat flakes with almond milk

350g raw buckwheat groats, soaked for
    one hour
6 dates, soaked
1 tablespoon raw cacao powder
1 teaspoon vanilla extract
¼ teaspoon cinnamon
pinch of salt

Rinse the buckwheat groats well until the water runs clear, then
drain well. Place the groats along with all the other ingredients into
a food processor and process until well mixed.

Line 2 dehydrator trays with baking paper and divide the
mixture between the trays, spreading out to a thickness of about
3mm. Dehydrate at 45°C for 6 hours or until dry to the touch. Peel
off the baking paper, flip over and dry for a further 2 hours until
crisp. Thickness and drying times are dependent on your preference
for how thick you want your flakes and how chewy or crisp –
experiment and see what works for you.

Break the dried buckwheat sheet into pieces and store in an
airtight jar, where they will stay fresh for at least a week.

Almond milk

150g blanched almonds, soaked overnight
450ml water

Blend together, preferably in a high-speed blender, until smooth.
Either use the milk as it is or strain through cheesecloth for a
smoother milk – however, if you choose to do this, you might want
to find a use for the nut residue. Biscuits, crackers and raw muesli
are three good options.

Sea vegetable salad ⓢ

Serves 4
25g dried dulse, roughly chopped
25g nori flakes
25g arame, soaked for half an hour, drained
    and rinsed
50g sprouted sunflower seeds
2 carrots, very finely shredded
2 celery stalks, very finely shredded
1 leek, white part only, very finely shredded
1 tablespoon tamari
1 tablespoon rice vinegar
1 tablespoon olive oil
4 handfuls of salad leaves

For the miso sauce
1 tablespoon ginger, grated
1 tablespoon horseradish, grated
2 cloves garlic, grated
2 tablespoons light miso
1 tablespoon sunflower oil
1 tablespoon tamari
4 sprigs of rosemary

To make the sea vegetable salad:
Toss all the ingredients except the salad leaves together.

To make the miso sauce:
Blitz all the ingredients except the sprigs of rosemary together,
adding a little water as necessary to make a pouring consistency.

Divide the salad leaves between 4 plates and pile the sea vegetable
salad on top, then spoon over the miso sauce and top with a sprig
of rosemary.

Apple, celery and walnut salad with almond mayonnaise ⓝ

Serves 4
2 large apples
1 large head of celery
24 walnut halves
1 tablespoon lemon juice
handful of parsley, chopped
2 heads of white or red chicory

For the almond mayonnaise
85g skinned whole almonds
150ml water
1 teaspoon wholegrain mustard
½ teaspoon salt
a good pinch of black pepper
150ml sunflower oil
1 tablespoon apple cider vinegar

<u>To make the salad:</u>
Quarter and core the apples and finely slice. Wash the celery stalks and chop into small pieces. Combine the apples, celery and walnuts together, and toss with the lemon juice and chopped parsley.

Break up the chicory and divide between 4 plates. Spoon the apple, celery and walnut mixture in the middle. Place a spoonful of almond mayonnaise in the centre of each salad.

<u>To make the almond mayonnaise:</u>
Place almonds in a blender or food processor and grind to a fine powder. Add half the water, along with the mustard, salt and pepper. Blend well, and then add the remaining water to form a smooth cream. With the blender running slowly, pour in the oil, blending until the mixture is thick. Add the vinegar and blend a minute longer. This keeps well in the fridge for 3 days.

Winter salad with flaxseed and chilli dressing

Salad can be grown throughout the winter – in the garden, in a greenhouse, in a window box and some varieties even on a windowsill. The choice is huge: rocket, mibuna, mizuna, winter purslane, mustard leaves, corn salad, butterhead lettuce, texsel greens, land cress, coriander, flat-leaf parsley, chervil, sorrel and baby leaves of kale are all excellent choices for a winter salad, and even if you cannot grow your own, there will be a variety to buy at your local farmers' market.

Place the leaves in a big bowl and toss through the flaxseed and chilli dressing.

Serves 4
For the flaxseed and chilli dressing
2 tablespoons flaxseed, soaked overnight in
    150ml carrot juice
1 small red chilli
1 tablespoon olive oil
1 clove garlic, crushed
2 tablespoons parsley, chopped

Blend all the ingredients together until you have a smooth dressing, adding a little water if necessary.

Six flavour soup ⓢ

Serves 4
1 fennel bulb
3 small carrots
6 celery stalks from the heart
2 cloves garlic
1 teaspoon honey
    to bring a little sweetness
1 tablespoon lime juice
    for the sour touch
1 chilli, finely chopped
    pungent, to add a zing
1 heaped tablespoon dark miso
    to add depth and roundness or umami
small handful of dulse, shredded
    salty, to bring out the flavours
large handful of alfalfa
    a little bitter kick
2 stoned umeboshi plums
    the finishing touch

Remove the outer leaves of the fennel, cut the bulb in half and finely slice. Peel the carrots and finely slice on the diagonal. Slice the celery and finely chop the garlic. In a bowl mix the honey, lime juice and chilli together. Add the vegetables and rub the marinade in well.

Divide the miso between 4 bowls and mix to a softer paste with a tablespoon of water in each. Divide the vegetables between the bowls, along with the dulse. Stirring well, fill the soup bowls with boiling water. Top each soup with alfalfa and half an umeboshi plum.

Potato and kimchi gratin

Serves 4
olive oil
1.2kg potatoes (King Edward or
    Desiree are good)
1 onion
4 tablespoons turnip kimchi
285ml vegetable stock
salt and pepper

Preheat the oven to 150°C/300°F/Gas mark 3.

Oil a large, shallow, ovenproof dish. Scrub and very finely slice the
potatoes, but do not rinse. Finely slice the onion and roughly chop
the kimchi.

   Arrange potato slices over the base of the dish, then cover with
the onion and half the kimchi. Add another layer of potato and the
remaining kimchi. Sprinkle generously with black pepper and a little
salt. Finish with a neat layer of potatoes that slightly overlap.

   Heat the stock and pour it over the potatoes. Brush the top with
olive oil and put it in the oven for about an hour or until tender; if
necessary, turn the oven up to make the top layer crisp and
golden brown.

Barley pilaf with winter squash, kale and red onions Ⓖ Ⓓ

Serves 4
5 tablespoons olive oil
water
4 red onions, finely sliced
1 carrot, finely chopped
2 celery stalks, finely sliced
225g barley
zest of 1 lemon
1 tablespoon thyme, finely chopped
600ml vegetable stock
350g butternut squash or crown prince
    in 1cm cubes
1 teaspoon cumin
½ teaspoon paprika
½ teaspoon salt
450g kale, coarse stems removed and
    roughly chopped
lemon juice
parsley
crème fraîche

Heat 3 tablespoons of the olive oil with the same amount of water and gently cook the red onion until soft. Add the carrot and celery and cook for a further couple of minutes, then add the barley. Stir well, then add the lemon zest, thyme and vegetable stock. Stir, cover the pan tightly and cook over a low heat for 45 minutes or until the barley is tender and all the liquid is absorbed.

   Whilst the barley cooks, toss the squash in the remaining oil with the cumin, salt and paprika and roast for 15–20 minutes in a hot oven.

   Steam the kale for 3 minutes, then stir the kale and squash into the barley. Heat through, adding a little extra stock if necessary, and serve with a splash of lemon, chopped parsley and a dollop of crème fraîche.

Roast broccoli with tahini dressing Ⓢ

Serves 4
3 heads of broccoli, cut into large florets
3 cloves garlic, finely diced
2 tablespoons olive oil
2 tablespoons of tamari
1 tablespoon lightly toasted sesame seeds

For the tahini dressing
3 tablespoons tahini
1 teaspoon ground cumin
juice of 1 large lemon
2 cloves garlic, crushed
½ teaspoon paprika
good pinch salt
3 tablespoons water

Heat the oven to 200°C/400°F/Gas mark 6.

Toss the broccoli with the garlic, olive oil and tamari and place
in a roasting tin. Roast the broccoli in the preheated oven
for 5 minutes.

Mix the tahini, cumin, lemon juice, garlic, paprika and salt
together in a bowl, then slowly mix in the water a little at a time
until you have a creamy dressing.

Pile the broccoli into a dish, pour over the dressing, scatter over
sesame seeds and serve.

Sourdough drop scones ⒢Ⓔ

Serves 4
125g rye leaven
125g spelt flour
pinch of salt
2 eggs, lightly beaten
2 tablespoons olive oil, plus a little extra

Beat all the ingredients together until you have a smooth batter that drops slightly reluctantly off the spoon.

Heat a heavy-based frying pan over a medium heat and smear lightly with a little olive oil. Drop tablespoonfuls of the mixture into the pan. After just a couple of minutes, when they are set and have bubbles on the surface, flip them over and cook for a minute or so longer until the second side is brown. Set aside in a warm place while you cook the rest.

....

A winter sourdough rye ⒢

225g rye flour
225g rye leaven
85g millet flakes
30g ground pumpkin seeds
30g sunflower seeds
2 tablespoons linseed
28g dulse, soaked and chopped
1 tablespoon spirulina
60g shelled hemp
1 tablespoon molasses

Heat the oven to 210°C/410°F/Gas mark 7.

Place all the ingredients together into a large bowl. With the addition of a little tepid water or a little extra flour, as necessary, mix together using your hands until soft, a bit sticky and well combined. Scrape any dough from your hands and wash them well.

Oil two small loaf tins, then, with wet hands, divide the dough in half and gently shape each piece in your hands into a loaf shape and lower into a tin. Flatten the dough with a spatula so it fits snugly into the tin, sprinkle over rye flour, cover well and leave in a warm place until double the size, roughly between 2–5 hours.

Bake in the preheated oven for about 40 minutes. Turn out onto a wire rack and cool.

Linseed crackers with hemp pâté

For the linseed crackers
175g linseed
285ml carrot juice

To make the linseed crackers:
Roughly grind the linseed, tip into the carrot juice, stir well and leave for 20 minutes.

Using a spatula or the back of a dessert spoon, spread the mixture thinly onto 2 baking paper lined dehydrator trays. Dehydrate for 8 hours at 45°C / 110°F. Flip the sheets over and peel away the paper, place back into tray and dehydrate until crispy. Break into pieces and serve with hemp pâté. Delicious also with baba ganoush, guacamole, hummus or any bean pâté. Store any leftover in an airtight glass jar for up to two weeks.

For the hemp pâté
225g shelled hemp seeds
550ml water
1 teaspoon salt
1 teaspoon cumin
¼ teaspoon chilli powder

To make the hemp pâté:
Place all the ingredients in a blender and blitz for a minute. Place into a pan and slowly bring to the boil, stirring all the time. The mixture will separate into 'curds and whey'. Simmer gently for 2–3 minutes until most of the liquid has evaporated. Place a piece of cheesecloth over a sieve sitting on a bowl and tip the mixture into the cloth. Gather up the cloth ends and tie up securely with a piece of string. Hang up over a bowl to drain overnight. Remove from the cheesecloth and refrigerate.

Chocolate hemp brownie with chocolate hemp sorbet ⒹⒺⓃ

For the chocolate hemp brownie
350g bitter dark chocolate broken into small
    pieces
350g butter, preferably unsalted
6 large eggs
350g rapadura sugar
175g ground almonds
85g shelled hemp seeds
20 x 30cm tin, buttered and lightly sprinkled
    with rice flour

Heat the oven to 180°C / 350°F / Gas mark 4.

To make the chocolate hemp brownie:
Combine the chocolate and the butter in a saucepan and melt
carefully, over a low heat, stirring all the time with a wooden spoon.
Beat the eggs and sugar together in an electric mixer until pale,
creamy and thick. Stir the chocolate mixture into the egg mixture.
Fold the almonds and hemp into the mixture and bake in the oven
for 20 minutes.

For the chocolate hemp sorbet
150g rapadura sugar
250ml water
100g bitter dark chocolate
60g raw cacao powder
100ml hemp milk (strained for smoothness)

To make the chocolate hemp sorbet:
Place the sugar and water in a saucepan and dissolve over a low heat,
then bring to the boil and boil for a few minutes. Remove from the
heat, cool slightly, then stir in the chocolate and dissolve. Whisk the
cacao powder into the hemp milk, then add to the syrup mixture.
Place the mixture in a container suitable for freezing and freeze
until slushy. Remove the mixture from the freezer and whisk until
smooth. Place back into the freezer and repeat the process two more
times, then freeze until ready to use. Alternatively, if you have an ice
cream maker, churn and then freeze until ready to use.

Mulled apple juice

2 slices root ginger
a stick of cinnamon
¼ teaspoon nutmeg, grated
¼ teaspoon cloves
2 star anise
1 bay leaf
a twist of finely pared lemon
a twist of finely pared orange
75cl bottle of apple juice
dash of brandy (optional)

Put the spices, bay and peel into a pan with half the apple juice,
bring to the boil and simmer gently for 5 minutes. Leave for the
flavours to develop, overnight or for a minimum of an hour. Strain,
add the remaining apple juice, warm through and serve. If you are
using brandy, add just before serving.

acknowledgements

Thank you to the most wonderful friends and family who support me in so many ways.

Special thanks to Peter Kindersley, John Lister, Charles Redfern and Urs Wild.

Love and gratitude to Polly Higgins for the forward; Romy Fraser, Diane Osgood, Miche Fabre Lewin and Sandra White for inspiring essays; Graham Challifour, Flora Gathorne-Hardy, Leo Zoltan and Adam Griffiths, whose images accompany mine.

I cherish the wonderful memories of Roger Hammond and Dragana Villinac who are greatly missed and to whom I owe much.

Deep appreciation to the Unbound team for their commitment and support.

A huge thank you to all the amazing growers who have inspired me over the years with an abundance of vibrant vegetables.

And finally, thanks to everyone who has shared preparing and eating food, along with stories reflecting their cultural traditions, around my kitchen table.

recipe index

almonds
    almond milk 255
    almond milk with rose and cardamom 154
    apple, celery and walnut salad with almond mayonnaise 257
    buckwheat flakes with almond milk 255
    carrot cake with hemp cream 205
    chocolate hemp brownie with chocolate hemp sorbet 265
    fig and chocolate smoothie 193
    Frisée, watercress and radicchio with Russet apples and walnuts 193
    lemon geranium cake 90
    prune, spirulina and almond smoothie 253
    sprouted seed salad 81
    strawberry breakfast 142
    strawberry smoothie 56
    summer berries with almond cream and breakfast scones 125
    winter cacao smoothie 57
apples
    apple, beetroot and ginger juice 253
    apple, celery and walnut salad with almond mayonnaise 257
    apple granola 194
    blackberry and apple juice 193
    mulled apple juice 266
    rosehip chutney 204
artichokes
    kimchi 203
asparagus
    dandelion, radish and asparagus salad 165
    quinoa with spring herbs and asparagus 84
barley pilaf with winter squash, kale and red onions 261
beans
    cassoulet 128
    potato, spinach and fava beans with coriander 199
    tempeh 183
    white bean soup 229
beech leaf noyau 92
beetroot
    apple, beetroot and ginger juice 253
    beetroot soup with fermented vegetables 82

pickled ginger 145
roast pumpkin and broccoli salad with beetroot and hemp 166
blackberries
blackberry and apple juice 193
blackberry vinegar 208
blueberries
autumn berry smoothie 57
blueberry tart 152
breads
wild garlic grissini 89
breakfast scones 125
sourdough rye bread 200
sourdough drop scones 263
tomato and garlic flatbreads 151
broccoli
roast broccoli with tahini dressing 262
roast pumpkin and broccoli salad with beetroot and hemp 166
buckwheat
buckwheat crackers 81
buckwheat flakes with almond milk 255
buckwheat pancakes 124
strawberry breakfast 142
butternut squash
baked butternut squash with spiced quinoa stuffing and roast red
    pepper dressing 198
barley pilaf with winter squash, kale and red onions 261
cabbage
rainbow salad 143
sauerkraut 202
cacao
buckwheat flakes with almond milk 255
cacao smoothie 57
chocolate hemp brownie with chocolate hemp sorbet 265
chocolate mousse 207
fig and chocolate smoothie 193
cakes
carrot cake with hemp cream 205
lemon geranium cake 90
carrots
carrot cake with hemp cream 205

    cassoulet 128
    linseed crackers 264
    kimchi 203
    radish, carrot, nettle and lemon juice 79
    rainbow salad 143
    sea vegetable salad 256
    six flavour soup 259
    spring tonic tart 90
    summer vegetable and pickled ginger sushi rolls 144
    warm kale salad with shiitake mushrooms 167
    white bean soup 229
cassoulet 128
celery
    apple, celery and walnut salad with almond mayonnaise 257
    wheatgrass, celery and ginger juice 79
    six flavour soup 259
chilli
    harissa 146
    pickled marsh samphire 149
    sweet chilli dipping sauce 145
    winter salad with flaxseed and chilli dressing 258
chocolate
    chocolate hemp brownie with chocolate hemp sorbet 265
    chocolate mousse 207
    fig and chocolate smoothie 193
chutney
    rosehip chutney 204
courgettes
    courgette noodles with harissa, tomatoes and flat-leaf parsley 146
crackers
    buckwheat crackers 81
    linseed crackers 264
dates
    buckwheat flakes with almond milk 255
    chocolate mousse 207
    date paste 152
eggs
    baked eggs with spinach 226
    mushrooms, wilted greens, poached egg and rye toast 126
    sorrel frittata 85
    spring salad 82
fennel

    fennel with nasturtiums 148

    six flavour soup 259

figs

    fig and chocolate smoothie 193

    garden salad leaves with fig balsamic dressing 195

frisée, watercress and radicchio with Russet apples and walnuts 195

garden salad leaves with fig balsamic dressing 195

ginger

    apple, beetroot and ginger juice 253

    wheatgrass, celery and ginger juice 79

gorse flower wine 91

granola

    apple granola 194

green pepper, tomato, celery, garlic and horseradish juice 193

green smoothie 56

green soup 83

harissa 146

hemp

    carrot cake with hemp cream 205

    chocolate hemp brownie with chocolate hemp sorbet 265

    rhubarb and hemp smoothie 79

    roast pumpkin and broccoli salad with beetroot and hemp 166

juices

    apple, beetroot and ginger juice 253

    blackberry and apple juice 193

    green pepper, tomato, celery, garlic and horseradish juice 193

    mulled apple juice 266

    radish, carrot, nettle and lemon juice 79

    red grape and spirulina juice 139

    red pepper, basil, celery and cucumber juice 139

    wheatgrass, celery and ginger juice 79

kale

    barley pilaf with winter squash, kale and red onions 261

    kale with sweet potatoes and hazelnuts 228

    pear, kale and echinacea smoothie 253

    warm kale salad with shiitake mushrooms 167

kefir 80

kimchi 203

    potato and kimchi gratin 260

lasagna

    nettle and spirulina lasagne 86

lemons

lemon geranium cake 90

radish, carrot, nettle and lemon juice 79

lime flower tea 155

linseed crackers with hemp pâté 264

mushrooms

mushrooms, wilted greens, poached egg and rye toast 126

warm kale salad with shiitake mushrooms 167

nasturtiums

fennel with nasturtiums 148

nettles

nettle and spirulina lasagne 86

radish, carrot, nettle and lemon juice 79

pears

pear, kale and echinacea smoothie 253

peas

pea soup 142

tempeh 183

pickled ginger 145

pickled marsh samphire 149

potatoes

potato, spinach and fava beans with coriander 199

potato and kimchi gratin 260

prunes

prune, spirulina and almond smoothie 253

quinoa

baked butternut squash with spiced quinoa stuffing, roast red pepper dressing 198

quinoa with spring herbs and asparagus 84

quinoa tabbouleh 227

radishes

dandelion, radish and asparagus salad 165

radish, carrot, nettle and lemon juice 79

redcurrant syrup 141

red grape and spirulina juice 139

red pepper

red pepper, basil, celery and cucumber juice 139

red pepper dressing 199

rhubarb

poached rhubarb 80

rhubarb and hemp smoothie 79

roast broccoli with tahini dressing 262

rose syrup 141

rosehip chutney 204

salads
 dandelion, radish and asparagus salad 165
 frisée, watercress and radicchio with Russet apples and
  walnuts 195
 garden salad leaves with fig balsamic dressing 195
 rainbow salad 143
 roast pumpkin and broccoli salad with beetroot and hemp 166
 sea vegetable salad 256
 sprouted seed salad 81
 spring salad 82
 tomato salad 165
 warm kale salad with shiitake mushrooms 167
 winter salad with flaxseed and chilli dressing 258
sauerkraut 202
sea vegetable salad 256
scones
 sourdough drop scones 263
 summer berries with almond cream and breakfast scones 125
smoothies
 berry smoothie 57
 cacao smoothie 57
 fig and chocolate smoothie 193
 green smoothie 56
 pear, kale and echinacea smoothie 253
 prune, spirulina and almond smoothie 253
 rhubarb and hemp smoothie 79
 strawberry smoothie 56
 summer smoothie 139
sorrel
 green soup 83
 sorrel frittata 85
 spring tonic tart 90
soups
 beetroot soup with fermented vegetables 82
 green soup 83
 pea soup 142
 red and yellow tomato soups with chive oil 196
 six flavour soup 259
sourdough
 a winter sourdough rye 263
 sourdough drop scones 263
spiced elderberry syrup 207

spinach
    potato, spinach and fava beans with coriander 199
spring tonic
    spring tonic tart 90
    spring tonic vinegar 92
sprouts
    sprout greens 69
    sprouted seed salad 81
strawberries
    strawberry breakfast 142
    strawberry smoothie 55
summer recipes
    summer berries with almond cream and breakfast scones 125
    summer smoothie 138
    summer vegetable and pickled ginger sushi rolls with red chilli dipping sauce 144
sweet chilli dipping sauce 145
sweet potatoes
    kale with sweet potatoes and hazelnuts 227
syrups
    redcurrant syrup 141
    rose syrup 141
    spiced elderberry syrup 207
tarts
    blueberry tart 152
    spring tonic tart 90
tempeh 182
tomatoes
    courgette noodles with harissa, tomatoes and flat-leaf parsley 146
    green pepper, tomato, celery, garlic and horseradish juice 193
    quinoa tabbouleh 227
    red and yellow tomato soups with chive oil 196
    tomato and garlic flatbreads 151
    tomato salad 165
turnips
    kimchi 203
vinegar
    blackberry vinegar 208
wakame
    white bean soup 229
wheatgrass
    wheatgrass, celery and ginger juice 79
wild garlic grissini 89

list of supporters

Clive and Jill Adams
Isobel Adams
Sarah Alhamad
Katherine Allen
    (with love from Sarah)
Fergus Anderson
Snjezana Aston
Naomi Baird
Luke Banfield
Linda Barlow
Vanessa Barlow
Katherine Barnett
Jenny Barrett
Susi Bascon
Delphine Bastien
Helen Bates
Beaufighter
Jayne Bedford
Kasia Bijak
Karen Booker
Lisa Bourboulis
Boutique Hotel Vivenda Miranda
    Lagos Algarve
Carrie Boysun
Geraldine Bradbury
Gilly & Roger Brewer
Joanna Brown
Peter Brown
Tania Brown
Sara Budd
Wesley Burden
Bernadette Bustin
Renata Byrne
Serena Calderisi
Silvia Campbell
Xander Cansell
Michael Caplan
Andrea Casalotti
Gary Chamberlain
Jack Chantler
Hao Chen
Jan Chen
Benjamin Chiad
Fleur Clackson
Nick Clifton-Welker

Alan Constantine
The Corbishleys
Murray Cordell
Hilary Cottam
Louise Court
Lisa Craig
Susan Curtis
Karl de Leeuw
Rorie Delahooke
Marie Derome
Trish Dickinson
Kirsten Disney
Les Dodd
Jane Dolan
Hans Dols
Sandie Draper
Paul Driver
Candida Dunford-Wood
Caroline Ede
Gareth Edwards
Kathryn Edwards
Renée Elliott
Laura Ellison
Aysen Ergene
Dulcie Faraway
Joan Fawcett
Mike Fisher
Sherry Forbes
Liz Ford
Yvonne Forsey
Geoff Fox
Isobel Frankish
Romy Fraser
Anna Freedman
Deborah Gallagher
Paula Gallardo
Mick Gander
Jennifer Gascoigne
Argus Gathorne-Hardy
Flora Gathorne-Hardy
Diane Godfrey
Alex Gooch
Joe Gooch
Jane Gooding
Charlotte Goodlet

Chrissy Gray
Adam Griffiths
Ivan Griffiths
Jason Griffiths
Martin Griffiths
Ben Griffiths & Jess Mealing
Karina Grippaldi
Sara Haglund
Catherine Hale
Jenny Hall Hall
Sonia Hammond
Michael J Hancock
Sara Hannan
Simon Hargreaves
Susan Harley
Rose Harris
Zena Harris
Carol Harvey
Ella Hashemi
Phil Haughton
Susanna Hawkins
Kerry Haywood
Jay & Christine Hennessy
Sarah JC Hennessy
Polly Higgins
Amy Hill
Sandra Hill
Dana Hirsch
Natalie Hogg
Nick Honey
Regan Hook
Zoe Howard
Tiffany Jesse
Alison Johnson
Fee Johnson
Terry Jones
Paulo Jorge de Oliveira Cantante
    de Matos
Sandor Katz
Ros Kennedy
Saffron Knight
Lesley Labram
Desmond Lambert
Chetna Lawless
Janet Lees
Chloe Leila
Orde Levinson
Miche Fabre Lewin
Rupert Lewis
Karen Lindley

Gail Lineham
Karen Livesey
Maddy Longhurst
Elspeth Lorriman
Lauren Lovatt
Carole Lovesey
Tamsin Loxley
Seonaid Mackenzie-Murray
Honor Mackley-Ward
Kerstin Maier
Martina Manna
Jane Manning of World Jungle
Deano Martin
Katy Martin
Ash Matadeen
Chris Mattos
John Peter Maughan
Federico Maya
Niki McCann
Margaret Mears
Jehanne Mehta
Jojo Mehta
Alice Meller
Tina Melvin
Liz Merrick
Bryony Middleton
Caroline Milford
Shipton Mill
Jos Mol
Nicola Møller
Lara Montgomery
Neil Monty-Smith
Claire Morris
Lisa Morris
Abby Mosseri
Erin Murphy
Lorraine Maddams Muth
Carlo Navato
Neal's Yard Remedies
David Neilson
Karen Newey
Gary Nicol
Glenda Nielsen
Siobhan Nolan
Jo Norcup
Marette O'Rourke
Aysegul Onat
Organico Realfoods
Diane Osgood
Jessica Oughton

Christine Page
Monica Perdoni
Jamie Pike
Michel Pimbert
Kathleen Pittman
Iain Plumtree
Philip Podmore
Barbara Pollard
Justin Pollard
Michelle Purse
Stephen Purse
Mandy Pursey
Jennie Pyatt
Hazel Radford
David Ratcliff
Sue Rayment
Susan Rayment
Charles Redfern
Jennifer Reid
Gillian Reynolds
Nate Richardson
Jackie Richmond
Tamsin Rickeard
Amanda Riley
Imogen Robertson
Gareth Rogers
Aquila Rose
Amanda Sander
Claudia Sartori
Roger Saunders
Vicki Savage
Dinam Sbardelott
Mr & Mrs B Schoenholzer
Chris Seeley
Stephen Shaw
Sheepdrove Trust
Carole Shorney
Juliet Simpson
Sarah Simpson
Elizabeth Sims
Jan Slimming
Sam Smit
Rich Smith
Jenny Sommerville
Anna Spanna
Ishah Speers
Erika Spooner
Jacqui Sread
Jessica Standing
Ulrike Stock

Jonathan Stocks
Tessa Stone
Jan Strassen
Zoe Strassen
Marion Strupp
Jackie Switzer
Deborah Tallis
Chris Taylor
Jean Taylor
Alison Telfer
Maddy Terrick
Danielle Texeira
Alice Theodorou
Hannah Theodorou
Andy Thesen
Anna Tilsley
Lizzy Tinley
Lindsay Trevarthen
Eric Trevino
Jane Trowell
Peter Turner
Sarah Turner
Della Tysall
Julia Van Berkel
Stephanie van der Liet
Bill and Susie van Marle
Gwen Vaughan
Richard Visick
Charlotte von Bulow
Sue Walker
Aleexj Wardie
Diana Warrings
Pat Welford
Mark and Morag Weston
Veronica Wheatley
Kate and Ashley Wheeler
Pip Whibley
Sandra White
Meredith Whitely
Benjamin Wilcox
Karin Wild
Marc Wild
Nadine Wild
Sarah Wild
Urs Wild
Vera Wild
David Wilsdon
Martyn Windsor
Elisabeth Winkler
Paulette Winwood

Chris Wood
Emma Wood
Hugh Dunford Wood
Jenna Marie Wright
Julia Wright
Janis Young
Gabriele Zoltan
Shahida Zubair

organico

Ecological small-scale farming and local food systems are key to
thriving networks of artisan producers and engaged citizens who
value the quality of traditionally-made foods.

Organico works directly with farmer-makers who care about the
soil, the food they grow and harvest, the people they work with and
the quality of their artisan products. From pasta and olives to rice
and tomatoes, the Organico way is to work with growers who love
what they do and to provide for people who love great-tasting food.

Our organic tomatoes are picked and grown in Tuscany – we can
even match a field to a can if we want – and then, over an intense
few days, they are harvested and processed by the same farmers who
have actually grown them.

Good food is about provenance, authenticity and linking the
health of the soil to our human health; linking the vitality of
ingredients to the way in which they are grown, and about kinship,
community and justice. This is the Organico approach.

www.organico.co.uk

neal's yard remedies

Neal's Yard Remedies has, since the very beginning back in 1981, encouraged a more natural, holistic way of health, beauty and wellbeing, through living in harmony with nature.

When we look to nature, we see a medicine cabinet full of extraordinary herbs and flowers, which have formed the basis of many modern medicines.

Many of these healing plants have therapeutic properties to help ease stress, boost health, improve skin conditions and benefit body, mind and mood. Herbs and essential oils are at the heart of everything we produce at Neal's Yard Remedies.

Today we grow many of our organic herbs ourselves, at our eco-factory in Peacemarsh, Dorset, and Sheepdrove Organic Farm, high on the Lambourn Downs in Berkshire. We support small farms and co-operative producers and know the origins of every herb and ingredient we use.

The FUTURE is in our hands: We believe in protecting this precious planet, for our future, our children's future and their children's future. The future lies in Soil, Not Oil!

www.nealsyardremedies.com

shipton mill

Fields of cereal grains swaying in the wind, stoneground milling and artisan baking form a very big part of our food culture heritage.

Shipton Mill produces a variety of flour that both master and home baker can use to bake products with a vibrant aroma, texture and flavour. The quality of flour is dependent on the choice of grain and the skill of the miller.

Organic and biodynamic growing systems produce a superior quality grain and choosing native, ancient and heirloom grain varieties is an important part of the stewardship of genetic diversity that contributes greatly to the richness of our natural environment.

The process of using stones to grind wheat into flour is an ancient tradition. Many of the health benefits of grain are maintained when flour is stoneground. The stones used stay cold, unlike industrial mills where the heat generated from the steel roller milling process destroys important nutrients.

The mill in Shipton Moyne Wood has been producing flour since the time of the Domesday Book. Today it is at the forefront of milling flours, using traditional grains and methods.

www.shipton-mill.com

vivenda miranda

Vivenda Miranda is set amidst some of nature's most outstanding beauty.

Nestled into the majestic cliffs above Porto de Mós beach in the western Algarve, the boutique hotel enjoys spectacular panoramic views of the sparkling Atlantic Ocean, dramatic coastline and endless sky. This former private home of a 17th century British noble family is surrounded by mature, colourful, natural indigenously planted Mediterranean gardens, which provide a secluded and ecologically aware paradise that breathes calm, tranquillity and integrity.

The Mirandus Restaurant, true to the origins of the word restaurant, is truly restorative. The kitchen brings culinary skills and traditions to the art of creating beautiful, healthy dishes from seasonal, organic and local produce that are good for you and the planet.

Vivenda Miranda supports and promotes organic and biodynamic farming as it is a regenerative agriculture. Their authentic artisan gastronomy features ingredients from organically reared animals, sustainable, locally caught and farmed seafood and plants grown locally in fertile, healthy soils. Through their relationships with local small-scale growers and artisan producers, cultural resilience and local food economies are strengthened.

www.vivendamiranda.com